This is a fascinating topic, so enjoy it! Reading and learning should be fun, engaging and it should leave you wanting MORE! So welcome to this piece of (highly unconventional) self development by

Martin Davies

KFC., RMN., B&Q., DhL., M&S.,

C&A., CPN., MRCCA., IBM.

ISBN:1985752700
ISBN-13:9781985752702

DEDICATION

Dedicated to all inhabitants of planet Earth who have caught some seriously bad STRESS INFECTIONS, often due to catching PAIN from seriously PAIN-FULL characters or PAINFUL events! May those of you who share this wonderful planet, who decide to complain, moan or strike out at those of us who are just trying to get on with our (already difficult) lives, please just go and …
GET A LIFE!

Thank you Marie Reilly for nagging me to do this.
Dedicated also to my children and wife who have
all experienced HUGE stress infections.

Bend.....but try not to break!

Important note: **The scenarios in this book can be adapted for work or life**, so feel free to extract the <u>messages</u> according to what situations are appropriate for you.... The above could be in WORK or at HOME or in LIFE. You may place yourself in any position you see, and indeed it can be helpful to place yourself in different places to see the different ways to view things, from different angles...from other people's perspectives. <u>**Stop and think!**</u>

Start as you mean to go on

May I suggest that before you start this book, consider it as a 'PERSONAL PROJECT' (if you are doing this for yourself), and create a personal journal. As I take you through this, imagine you are on a course, taking notes as things pop into your head. Use this journal constantly, even keeping it beside your bed to jot things down. This is YOUR project...YOUR time...so let's make the most of it

Let us start with our different 'heads'

All of us, throughout each day, move through a series of 'characters', depending on who we are with, where we are, what we are doing or how we are feeling.

Some of these *internal characters* are good for us, however some are not so helpful and may be a PAIN to both ourselves and to others. We move in and out of these all day, every day, mostly without even noticing. If we don't notice who or what is in our head, how can we learn to control them (particularly the 'heads' that cause us pain or discomfort)? Consider the different characters you move in and out of, and maybe even write down:

- List what you are aware of being like when you are "not good" (at work or at home)?
- List what you are like when you are "on top of the world" (you may need to think back 20 years!)?

Getting filled with PAIN

We all absorb a constant stream of 'stuff' throughout each day. Whether this is via reading a text, watching a programme on the TV, listening to a friend or colleague talking about something, or simply by encountering various events that float by us each and every day. Some of these events make us laugh, some just a smile, some may provoke a frown or make us upset. Each of these events *move us into a different character state*. We don't even need any of these *outside triggers* to provoke a change in us, we are perfectly capable of altering our psychological state by thinking something, eating something or acting in a particular way: we are often at the mercy of our own THOUGHTS, FEELINGS and BEHAVIOURS. We can change these to feel better.

Triggers that change us into 'somebody else'

How often do we see an injustice, and feel angry because of the unfairness. While we are in that 'INJUSTICE HEAD' we become opinionated, animated and feel a sense of resentment. Or perhaps we see two children playing happily, and feel their happiness, as it reminds us of a more innocent past. Perhaps we are spoken to in a nasty manner by someone at work, and bottle up the rage or the sadness. All of these 'triggers', whether from outside or from within ourselves, provoke us into different 'character' states, each character *behaves* differently, *feels* a range of emotions and *thinks* quite differently from each other. Feeling good, great, happy or wonderful is not the problem. It is when we are angry, resentful, miserable, helpless or hopeless that we become filled with PAIN...and start to SPREAD that pain to those around! We have become, a **CARRIER**! All of us are 'carriers' at times, 'spreading' our own pain, not just to those around us, but spreading it **INTO** our own selves: our thoughts get worse, eventually our emotions reflect what we think and it changes our entire behavior: we don't need outside triggers, we can do it ourself!

PAINFUL people are *PAIN-FULL*

I remember one of these people in one of my courses. Within two minutes of sitting down, she had *'infected'* everyone on each side of her (and she hadn't even opened her mouth!). The **non-verbal language** was loud and VERY clear...

The infections (notice this is *plural: several viruses were present in this one person!*) spread even quicker when she started talking! We are ALL capable of spreading pain, as we are ALL carrying around pain, at times in our lives. The difference is that some people are AWARE, <u>they have the INSIGHT</u> to either control it, or take it somewhere else, while others simply DUMP THEIR PAIN onto whoever they encounter! Perhaps then, the **important ingredients** here are....

<u>INSIGHT, AWARENESS, RESPECT</u> and <u>CARE</u>.

INSIGHT: Simply the *willingness* to take a look at oneself, to be prepared to consider our own part in things, is one of the basic building blocks to developing **AWARENESS**. Without insight or awareness, we trundle through life oblivious as to the *effects we may be having on others around us*. No doubt some of you readers will be immediately aware of certain people you may have encountered who are like this? Sometimes we may not have such awareness due to the lack of CARE.

CARE: How much do we care about the effects we are having on a) ourselves, and b) others? Without sufficient care we say whatever we want, do whatever we want, act in whatever way we want, with no regard to the consequences. Consider:

- Care for ourselves: What we eat, how we talk to others, how we conduct ourselves, how we behave socially, and how we treat ourselves?
- Care for others: Showing care, giving care, protecting others and having a social conscience. Maintaining a morality that is respected? Care is linked to RESPECT.

These INGREDIENTS provide us with: **The ability to CHANGE**

Without **insight** or **care**, it becomes too difficult (and impossible for some) to **change** in any way. Those without these ingredients may not only fight change, but also sabotage it for others. Some of us **used** to have the ability to change, **used** to have insight and considerable determination to change, but these have been *'hoovered'* out due to chronic distress. (*There are however, some people, who are simply difficult people due to their nature*!)

DEFINITION OF RESPECT:

Having regard for the feelings, wishes or rights of others, whether you know them or not, like them or not, agree with them or not.

PUBLIC HEALTH WARNING!

THERE IS A SERIOUS DROPPING OF RESPECT, CARE, INSIGHT AND AWARENESS IN HUMANITY!

Have you noticed how many people are simply not aware of their own rudeness or discourtesy in public? Consider how people use their mobile devices with other people present, how some people talk so loudly that everyone can hear, how some use social media to intimidate or bully others? Add to this general dropping of standards, ALCOHOL, and you see the high rates of aggressive behaviours, antisocial (and often child-like) attitudes displayed in public. It may be tempting to blame all this on the 'younger generation', but in fact it may be older people that also contribute to this lowering of public standards. We only need to look at the wars and conflicts around the globe, and the dreadful lives that some (mostly innocent) people have to endure, to see the other end of this scale. WHAT IS HAPPENING TO US?

The STRESS VIRUS breeds rapidly where there is strife and conflict! Yet it is also part of our fundamental human design: it is there all the time, and in small doses is perfectly ok.

The STRESS VIRUS under the microscope

The STRESS VIRUS:

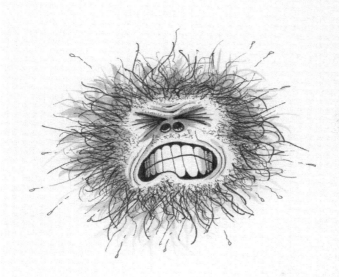

(<u>Latin</u>: *JOYUS STRANGULATUS*)

We ALL catch this virus and we ALL have it in our system. Anyone that tells you that they "...*never get stressed*...." is a **CORPSE!** Stress is part of what we need to get up in the morning; the problems only arise when we accumulate TOO MUCH of it, for TOO LONG. So accepting that 'STRESS' is normal is a good place to start. Understanding it, and not believing the myths and misunderstandings of it just being "BAD" is vital to coping better with it. I will go through this a little later.

Some people are obviously infected with a HIGH DOSE:

These are easy to spot! They have accumulated a LARGE STRESS INFECTION for too long and are not managing it particularly well. Such individuals (carriers) are highly likely to **SPREAD** it to others via *outbursts* and *emotional vomiting!* It is important for such highly infected people to not only listen to what others may be telling them, but to become more aware of what they are doing, and why?

The STRESS VIRUS can MUTATE:

Big STRESS INFECTIONS can be pretty awful, especially if the infection goes on and on. It is perfectly capable of *mutating* and provoking a whole range of symptoms such as tiredness, low mood, restlessness, physical pain, poor sleep, weight change, and worse. It is therefore SO important to catch it early, recognize it and step in with some kind of 'inoculation' to reduce the inflammation! INSIGHT helps us do this. Previous infections should help to teach us to pick up the early signs quicker.

It only takes ONE to spread it!

Imagine working with someone like this every day! Or being managed by such a person! *What about going home to sleep with a similarly infected individual?* it simply HAS to have an effect, and it may not be for the general good of the family or workplace team. Some people are simply not AWARE, or maybe don't CARE?

The poor VICTIMS who have PAIN dumped on them....

I met this particular individual in a GP surgery, and watched how they, within 3 seconds, infected the poor patients! The unfortunate patient only wanted some help, some assistance or some information and received a ***forked tongue***-lashing! Perhaps the receptionist was the poor victim of circumstance herself, <u>but this does not excuse such catastrophic attitudes</u>.

"Why do so many have a problem with mental health?"

All too often still, people assume the worst sorts of predjudices based on lack of knowledge, experience or understanding. What century do we live in that some STILL hold awful myths and peddle misbeliefs!

The HOOVER!

The *HOOVER* of work and life....

Whether it is work, life, relationships or circumstances, there seems to be a large vacuum cleaner SUCKING THE GOODNESS OUT OF US at times! Modern life seems to want MORE from us. Work, due to cutbacks and change demands more and MORE from its workforce, whilst often rewarding those above us. Relationships can be very demanding, and if we get wrapped up in the materialistic side of life. Unless you have a large bank account, the expectations can be overwhelming. Children WANT more, and they want it NOW, and it has to be the LATEST or most EXPENSIVE thing! But things have changed in recent years, it has got worse...

The new TURBO HOOVER....

We want more THINGS quicker (and they must be as good as others, or if not, BETTER!). The LATEST car, a PRIVATE NUMBERPLATE, a LABEL outfit....all sucking the goodness out of our bank accounts to feed our ego! Work is more demanding with less time and more deadlines, and some of us **_MUST_** be available _IMMEDIATELY_ . The TURBO-HOOVER can empty us!

Having demands made upon us is good and healthy.

A little bit of stress is OK, even good for you.....

It is even enjoyable, IF you enjoy your work and are interested in it then stress in small to medium doses is normal, good and is required to have a fulfilling life. DON'T KNOCK IT – we ALL need 'stress' to get up in the morning and to deal with life. The chemistry going on in our bodies that create stress, in small doses, is good. Without it we are corpses! Maybe we are misjudging it.

We all, at times, have jobs that can be repetitive and boring (doing tasks that we see no point in, but MUST be done). This is made

worse if we are not interested in our work, or do not have good co-workers to bounce off at times. Modern workplaces can be filled with 'MUST DO's': You MUST do it by noon, it MUST be done on the pink, green and blue forms, it MUST be done according to a particular formula, it MUST hit this target, it MUST be done MY way etc. etc. etc.!!!

Too many 'MUST DO's' is draining, and there is a name for this....

Many workplaces are now **MUSTERBATING** their staff! <u>Prolonged MUSTERBATION is bad for your health!</u> Thinking beyond work, LIFE can be MUSTERBATORY: *Must* have a new car, *must* have the latest phone, *must* have an orange skin, *must* have a car with a BIG exhaust pipe, *must* have a conservatory bigger than our neighbours, *must* have, **MUST have**, *MUST HAVE*...newer, bigger, latest, more expensive! The demands on poor parents are becoming impossible. Young children are now so concerned with **HAVING THING**S that are as good as, or better than their friends things, that their view of the world is becoming so **UNREALISTIC!**

TRIBALISM !

Tribalism is often more apparent in the workplace, where people start protecting their mugs, labeling their milk in the fridge and using badges or clothes to SHOW their 'tribe'! More tribalism occurs in teams that do not trust each other. But this behavior has existed in people since prehistory: within family gatherings there are also tribalistic behaviors, within groups of friends and between couples....sometimes it can help us differentiate between different groups, but sometimes it can cause CONFLICT, unnecessary COMPETITION and WALLS START GETTING BUILT! Beware what part you may be playing to either break barriers down, or being part of the construction team!

Hierarchy and tribalism can breed discontent...

The best workplaces do not have a traditional hierarchy structure; they have a 'flat' structure that allows easy access to all on a first name basis. Many organisations, particularly BIG or TRADITIONAL places ADORE things like RANK, STATUS, POSITION, POWER and MONEY, with the uniforms and badges to suit! Talking of SUITS: the SIZE of the STRIPE on a suit can be VERY IMPORTANT to some!

There are difficult people around!

Dealing with difficult people can be.....difficult!

We can all be 'difficult' at times, but some are experts! Some of us are good at cooking or baking cakes or playing a musical instrument, while others are GOOD AT INTIMIDATING others. They USE their (often well-honed skills) to MAKE others do what THEY want. Often loud, brash or confrontational on the outside, but actually extremely inadequate individuals inside. Inadequate people do not know how to use good communication, self-control, dignity, respect and care very well, so tend to try and FORCE their own agenda onto others, and get louder if they don't get their way. They want things THEIR way – it's the ONLY way!

Good team working is about sharing the burdens, being open and helpful when possible, and creating an atmosphere of empowerment to all. Good teams do things THAT COST THE ORGANISATION NOTHING: they say "Hi", or "Hello....good morning". They offer to get a cup of tea or occasionally bring in biscuits. Conflicts are dealt with amicably. How your work team?

The STRESS VIRUS starts infecting your THOUGHTS and your MIND!

In larger (more unhealthy) doses, the virus can easily trigger some pretty unpleasant thoughts which, if not stopped, can easily become a torrent of horrible 'inner dialogues'. These, in turn infect your emotions and feelings, turning you into a walking seething beast! A small infection of the mind can easily be disguised by a smile (no-one notices what is going on inside), while a BIG infection starts to show in people's faces, tone of voice or behaviours! Uh-oh...the virus may be spreading to others!

The virus can spread in teams...

Easily spread in groups of people, be it the team you work in, the family you live with, or the friends you come into contact with...the STRESS VIRUS can become an EPIDEMIC, infecting lots of people in close proximity! The potential for spreading **PAINFUL stuff is even higher now, with the use of SOCIAL MEDIA!** Creating FEAR (with individuals, within a family, at work or in society) has always been an efficient way of manufacturing a perfect breeding ground for the stress virus. Fear or pain SPREADERS are often inadequate, unhappy or resentful people who themselves, get a kick out of spreading their own (inner) pain and watching it blossom

Time is a problem.....

There are certain people (whom you could probably name) that you daren't ask: "How are you?" for fear of being held hostage for several hours! Some people just have no awareness as to the pain they are causing (Lack of INSIGHT), or they simply are not aware of the effects they are having on YOU (and maybe don't CARE anyway). Yet, if time is SO precious, how come we waste so much of it in pointless meetings?

The pointless meetings...

I actually went to this meeting, and they argued about the "biscuit issue" for over 40 minutes!!! At the end of this time, they decided (in their wisdom) to "...put it on the next agenda"! No wonder we can lose the will to go on when meetings become so pointless, and some people so petty. These may be highly intelligent individuals... but with very little EMOTIONAL INTELLIGENCE.

So it is NO WONDER that we can catch THIS virus:

The ANGER virus

(Latin: *FRUSTRATUS MAXIMUS*)

Bottling up FRUSTRATIONS and having to keep it all inside! The times when we feel ANGRY or HELPLESS or have to talk in ways that simply COVER UP how we REALLY feel, or behave as if nothing is wrong, can become excruciating! Anger is part of being human, it is how we deal with it and what we do with it that matters. Some of us have internal characters that manage our anger well, whilst others simply blow a gasket or hit out.

Another virus that can cause HUGE amounts of PAIN is ...

The ACADEMIC virus

(Latin: *ANUS RETENTICUS*)

Some people are just too clever! I have a feeling that there is a LEVEL OF CLEVERNESS that, if exceeded, some lose their social skills (if they ever had them)! Have you noticed that some 'clever people' are indeed, VERY CLEVER, but can't seem to bring themselves to say "Hello" or politely ask "How are you?".

Eventually, due to becoming infected with many viruses, you may catch...

The MISERY virus

(<u>Latin</u>: *SUICIDUS EVENTUALIS*)

This is when you see folk coming in, looking pretty worn down, and saying:" *"What's the point....no-one cares...they're all out to SHAFT you...wish I could retire...and I'm 23!"*. People wandering around, looking fed up, feeling ground down, maybe even becoming quite obstructive, dismissive or resentful, and maybe not knowing what to do. A sad state of affairs and an atmosphere which may become pretty toxic at home or at work. Being infected with all these viruses can have a devastating effect not only on ourselves, but on those we encounter.

Imagine going to a MEETING OF ALL THE VIRUSES!

A meeting of _all_ the viruses!

But these meetings DO happen! How often do we (at work meetings, or family gatherings) HOLD IN WHAT WE WOULD LIKE TO SAY OR DO! But, what we would LIKE to say is perhaps aggressive, rude, insensitive or downright unacceptable. What we would like to DO (rant or gesture or poke an eye out) would be an instant cause for dismissal! So, we fib, lie or cover up our REAL sentiments. It is maybe time to consider a theory of mine over the next few pages, about all this BOTTLED UP STUFF....

The SHOPPING TROLLEY theory!

As soon as you are awake, before you are even up, you start each day with an EMPTY SHOPPING TROLLEY, pushing it through the day **COLLECTING STUFF that you cannot possibly say or do**:

Saying: "Morning, lovely to see you!" (But inside thinking: "Damn, _they're_ here…. That's just spoiled my day!")

Smiling in a meeting (But inside wanting to poke the eye of that colleague or tell them to take a walk on a motorway!)

Saying: "Oh that's really helpful" (But inside thinking: "You pathetic toad…. Why are you wasting my valuable time!")

So, each day, saving up STUFF that you cannot possibly say or do.

So where do you take your STUFF...

....at the end of the day....

You've got it – HOME! At home, if you have a partner, THEY have their OWN TROLLEY! If you have children, THEY have THEY'RE trolley! All meet in a nice big CRASH! Emptying our trolleys onto each other: what a great start to the evening eh! But what if you live alone – no one to empty your trolley on? Well, that's easy...you take it all back into work the next day to collect more!

So, my IMPORTANT QUESTION TO YOU is this:

"Have you got the means to regularly

empty your trolley?"

You may take that as and how you wish! If you consider the person whom I described as 'PAIN-FULL' at the beginning, they do not appear to have a TROLLEY, *they have a TRUCK*! This person has not emptied their trolley for a long time! So consider:

- "What are you doing?" (to yourself, or to others)
- "What are you NOT doing...that might help empty your trolley more regularly?"

This is where the significance becomes clear, regarding your INTERESTS in life. Consider.....

- **A T.V. DOES NOT EMPTY A TROLLEY**
- **A MOBILE PHONE DOES NOT EMPTY A TROLLEY**
- **A COMPUTER DOES NOT EMPTY A TROLLEY**
- **ALCOHOL SIMPLY ANAESTHETISES US!**

Perhaps, more worryingly, what are young children doing (or NOT doing) to dilute or reduce their own built up tensions? How many people are GLUED to their mobile devices, addicted to that screen or shut down from REAL LIFE?

REAL LIFE is what REAL HUMAN BEINGS need more of, particularly now, in this world of increasing technology, a world which is becoming more Unreal. It is here to stay, and we need it...but how much are we now ADDICTED to it?

How COMPLETELY INSANE are our communication systems at work...

The joy of modern communication......

Family time is rapidly becoming 'FAMILY FISHBOWL' time! Unless you have created, *from the very start*, a system that reduces such scenarios as above, it is extremely difficult to change people's social behaviours, particularly if THEIR MOBILE PHONE IS WELDED INTO THEIR HANDS! Maybe we should stop and ask ourselves: "Do we care?". The **GLASS SCREEN**, whether it is the one on the living room or bedroom wall, or the one on the desk, or the one in your hand, is capable of taking you over, completely.

Lack of concentration can lead to missing things....

As our concentration gets worse, we can easily **not see** what is directly in front of us. Staring at a mobile phone can cause us to become oblivious to what is around. When we are feeling overwhelmed, we can also stop taking things in. This is when mistakes can be made, clumsiness sets in and our EMOTIONAL INTELLIGENCE becomes blurred and less sensitive. We stop seeing!

Some people, when pushed too far, just become a bit
ODD...

We can't quite put our finger on what is amiss, but we start to get
a feeling that the person has changed. If you are an 'important
person', and have an office, you can maybe shut yourself away
and no-one notices! Often, we can *put up an image* for those we
encounter in the day, but at night *the true self* emerges (much to
the consternation of those we share the home with!).

But some people just fall off the edge...

Some of us hit a point at where we become very unprofessional, or lose the plot completely. Perhaps we suddenly (even though it has built up over time) act a bit 'strange' or noticeably weird. What a shame that we did not catch this earlier, or that nobody else felt able to step in and say something, or help. **This can happen to anyone**. No-one is immune from the stress virus. You may wish to deny it or cover it up, but we can all succumb to it.

Anyone is at risk of becoming overwhelmed....

It can be very surprising as to how many people think they are completely IMMUNE to the stress virus and its complications. No-one is fully immune and it CAN happen to ANYONE! Remember: only a CORPSE does not get stressed! Some are just good at disguising it. I have met many a 'professional person' who is badly infected, but unable or unwilling, to acknowledge it.

When staff get together…..

So when there is a staff gathering or a break at work, what do we do? Often the first thing many now do, is pick up their mobile phone (and thus detach from those around them). But if we do actually talk, we are often indulging in a GROUP MOAN! Complaining about him, her, this and that…or perhaps what should be different or what ought o be changed to 'make things better'. Thus creating a further SWAMP OF MISERY for the viruses to breed in! Having a good moan is healthy, but constantly?

So what does it take to SIMPLY GET YOU INTO WORK.....

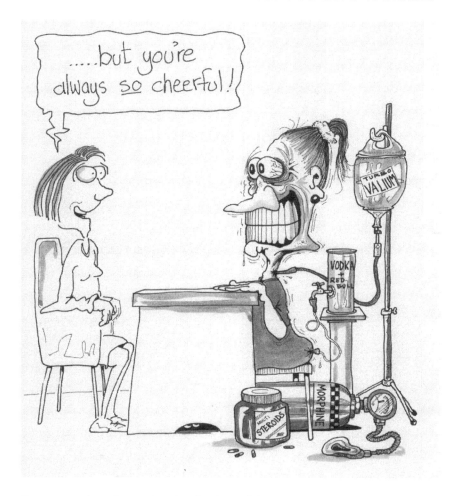

For some, it takes a heck of a lot of 'something' to get us up and keep us going through the day. Unfortunately, this 'something' may be a range of items that are not that good for us, or worse: are extremely BAD for us! How often do you see young teenagers drinking (so-called) 'Energy' drinks (you know the ones in the RED can or with the MONSTER size cans!). You may see a lot of adults doing this too? More commonly, HUGE drinks of coffee, loads of sweet cakes or crisps or fizzy drinks and various 'medications'.

The easiest thing to do is....

We all, to some extent indulge in a bit of this, but all too often we deny, to ourselves as well as those around us, things that may be difficult to admit to. Preferring perhaps, to hope that it all passes. Nobody likes 'bad stuff', and the tendency to sweep it all under the carpet is perfectly understandable... but that carpet can get pretty full of 'stuff' that has been topped up over years!

Emptying our trolley on the first person we meet...

At the end of the day

All too often we may **DUMP** our *accumulated stuff* on the first person we encounter when we get home. This is when the arguments may start! Maybe it is time to consider a DIFFERENT way to end the day.....or a different place to park our trolley (away from home)...or to partially empty it before we get home? What is the end of YOUR day like? Too much 'stuff' accumulating in that trolley of yours?

What do you do to RELAX at home after a hard day....

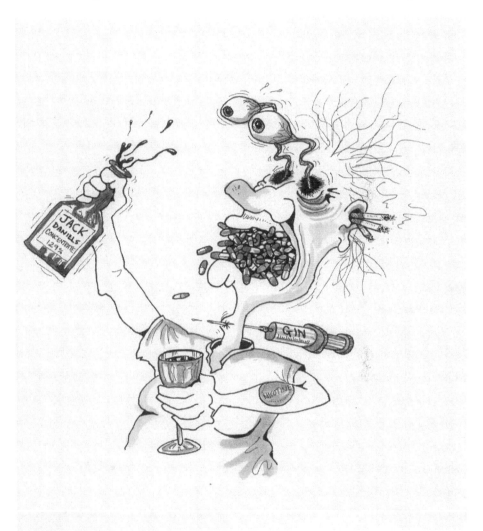

Alcohol can be the first thing we turn to, simply to *'calm the nerves'* or *'lift the mood'* (which alcohol, in large quantities does <u>NOT</u> do – it is likely to do the opposite!). Perhaps you just collapse in a heap in front of the T.V. or lock yourself away with your best friend: your MOBILE PHONE...your little world of unreality... placing yourself in that fishbowl that says: "KEEP OUT". Maybe it is time to consider some little changes?

Just when you thought it was safe to go to bed...

More stress! More demands and more 'MUST DO's'! More expectations and unrealistic requests push you into another corner.... creating a PERFECT BREEDING GROUND for more viruses! Or, perhaps you may be thinking "If only!" Bedtime is not always the restful place that we would like it to be. How often do we go to bed, with our BEST FRIEND: yes, it's that MOBILE PHONE again! We KNOW that using a screen before bed DOES have an effect on quality of sleep. Pause for thought!

Once the lights go out, our brain kicks in again...

Mulling through the events of the day or what you're going into tomorrow...so SLEEP is shallow, intermittent or certainly not restful, as it should be. We also know that the majority of children go to bed with their MOBILE PHONE; there is nothing like the *brain-wave-disturbing light* of a screen to disrupt normal sleep, as well as checking on all the social media to keep a brain alert! Many younger people set their phone alarms to waken them through the night, to check on all the various apps. Once IN you then PARTICIPATE. Marvelous for the health of a young and tired developing brain!

What price is "SUCCESS" then...?

Sometimes we may lose sight of what is actually important and we may become focused entirely on money, power, status, rank, what the neighbours might think, and generally 'keeping up appearances'... not the happiest or most rewarding ways to live, unless you are on your own (which is most likely where you may end up). In this modern age of impressing people, or catching the dreaded **AFFLUENZA** VIRUS, our ability to take the reality test may diminish: filling our lives with stuff that isn't actually REAL (digital friendships/digital conversations/digital lifestyles/digital 'mental foods'). We may easily detach ourselves from REAL (and often more satisfying) things that would REALLY make us more happy.

The daily battles....

The daily battles can start before you are even dressed, particularly if you have young children). Then you may have the daily 'battle' of commuting to work! Then the 'battle' with colleagues, the photocopier or printer! Then the 'battle' home, the 'battle' on getting through the front door, the evening 'battles' with partner or children, the bedtime 'battle'! Many of these battles – most of them unnecessary, but all of them exhausting, can be changed, but some can't be.

It is important to UNDERSTAND the PATTERN!

Every day, we each move UP AND DOWN...some days further UP and some days further DOWN. **THERE IS A PATTERN** to all of this that has consequences, some good and some not so.

UNDERSTANDING THE PATTERN is extremely important:

- WHAT level we are at (and where OTHERS are too)
- To understand the POTENTIAL CONSEQUENCES of where it can lead, unless we step in and DO something.
- To be AWARE WE NEED TO COME BACK DOWN or we will suffer more, and to learn from the signs we show.
- To have some AIMS and to PLAN ahead: create a strategy or at least to ber AWARE.

TERMINOLOGY: We are constantly under pressure, even as we sleep: the pressures of gravity, and the universe are pressures constantly exerted upon us, affecting our metabolism, blood pressure and brain functioning. Pressure is an engineering word, referring to FORCES. Nature and all the contents of our world are under constant pressure, constantly changing forces: plants have to TOLERATE forces and pressures of nature (weather, wind, rain, sun, temperature). They NEED this, as it helps them become STRONGER. These pressures and forces are all part of the STRESS that nature is under: it makes things STRONGER and more RESILIENT. As humans, we live in the same world, under the same pressures (or 'STRESSES') that also help us become stronger. No day is the same, but there are PATTERNS to nature that all have CONSEQUENCES for the inhabitants of this planet. Understanding these words and terms is important, or we may misinterpret something and come to a (misguided) meaning.

So, in summary:

- **PRESSURE is normal** – we need it, it makes us strong. Too much can be damaging.
- **STRESS is an engineering term** relating to the pressures that are put upon us. It is NORMAL and we need it. Too much can make us ill.
- **Anxiousness is NORMAL.** Being anxious is necessary and healthy. Too much anxiousness, for too long can lead to ill health.
- **Anxiety is an ILLNESS.** It is not normal to be in a state of anxiety.

So some words commonly used that we may think are 'medical' terms are not, they are engineering terms: words such as PRESSURE, TOLERANCE, and STRESS. Some words are mis-used and infer 'bad' meanings, such as ANXIOUS. Anxiousness is normal and passes. Large and prolonged doses of anxiousness can lead to OVER PRESSURE, which can be INTOLERABLE and lead to POOR RESILIENCE, thus leading to health problems such as ANXIETY and DEPRESSION. There are a range of stages that we move through from the moment we waken up. These stages create a PATTERN.

UNDERSTANDING THIS PATTERN, THE TERMINOLOGY, AND HOW EACH STAGE LINKS WITH THE OTHER, HELPS US TO MAKE SENSE OF WHAT CAN BE A CONFUSING PICTURE., WHICH CAN LEAD TO MORE (UNECESSASY) WORRY, FEAR AND FURTHER MISINTERPRETATIONS OF WHAT OUR MIND AND BODY ARE ACTUALLY TELLING US.

Terminology?

Engineers are used to measuring *forces*, *pressures* and *tolerances*. Building materials are all built to a very specific (and measureable) tolerance: steel girders are *meant* to bend slightly, just as bridges are *meant* to move and sway. The trouble is, humans are not all the same: we each have different tolerances, each cope differently with pressures. So we are using engineering words for humans, which are NOT easily measured, and are all different. We cannot use specific tolerance measurements for things in nature either: every tree is different, and each reacts differently to different pressures put upon it. So the words 'STRESS', and 'TOLERANCE' and 'PRESSURE' are not exact in humans or nature, but they are in engineering. We need 'stress' and 'pressure'.

But we have adopted these words, and unfortunately apply them incorrectly much of the time. How often do we hear: "I've been signed off work with stress." Or "This meeting gives me SO much anxiety!" Both phrases are incorrect – if anyone was to be off work due to "stress", then we should ALL be off, EVERY DAY! It is not stress we are off work with, it is something else. A meeting may make someone very anxious, but this is quite different from experiencing ANXIETY. We need to understand more, so this next section is aimed at trying to clarify the PATTERN and the TERMINOLOGY.

If we don't understand the words, we will inevitably misinterpret them, which can lead to excessive worry, fear and make things worse than they actually need to be. KNOWLEDGE IS POWER!

Are you a **swimmer** in the **pool of stress**?

Think of STRESS a bit like a swimming pool: a little paddle in the shallow end is often pleasant (even for people who can't swim). As you get in deeper, you need more skills about you to keep afloat. Even the best swimmer can't stay in the water indefinitely: they need to come out for a break! Being in the deep end is fine, if you have all the capabilities to swim there. But if anyone stays there for too long, without breaks and 'time out'...they will sink!

Before anything starts, we are asleep, in bed, at our most relaxed.

From waking we progress up a **range of levels**...

THE SLEEP ZONE

So, you are in your sleep...your body and mind are at their greatest point of relaxation. Your body systems (e.g. respiratory – cardiovascular – muscles etc.) are in a very slow and relaxed state. Your brainwave activity is in 'sleep' mode! In this zone ALL humans are at their most relaxed state. ZZZzzzzzzz

THE LOW FUNCTION ZONE: As soon as your body wakens, a release of a range of chemical 'messengers' starts to alert your system....but you are not fully awake!

The alarm clock goes off or your sleep comes to a natural end. Your body is moved to **THE LOW FUNCTION ZONE.** Your body does what it has always done since prehistoric times: it releases a range of 'chemical messengers' into the body and mind to bring it out of sleep. But this is not the time of day to read a report or fix the roof – you can barely talk! You are in a **LOW functioning state**, only able perhaps to think of going to the toilet or getting a cup of tea. These chemical messengers are the same substances that cause a panic attack, but they are in such LOW quantities, they simply (but slowly) bring your mind and body out of sleep. You NEED this...it GETS YOU UP...these chemicals are in part, 'stress' chemicals. So stress is good, in small amounts.

THE FUNCTIONING ZONE

Each of us stays in the 'LOW FUNCTION ZONE' for different periods of time: some only for a few minutes, whilst others, quite normally, stay there for ages. We are all different! After a time, your body's *alerting system* increases its effect, releasing more chemicals into this ever-wakening human body. You are fully awake, perhaps already having breakfast and having a wash or getting dressed. You are also thinking clearly about what you are doing and the day ahead.

THE FUNCTIONING ZONE: Your brain is starting to work, and your body is getting warmer (still not ready for work yet, but slowly getting into gear).

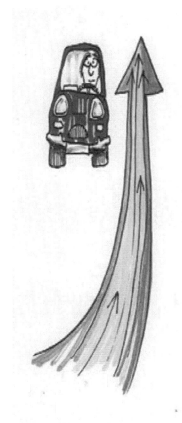

THE FULLY ALERT ZONE: All your systems are warmed up and ready for the battles of the day!

You are up and getting to work, all washed and dressed nicely. Your body's alerting system fully functioning: **YOU ARE COOKING BABY** and well on the way to the next zone. Without all these alerting chemicals (stress) you'd still be in bed! Stress is GOOD and gets you into a more functioning place to battle the day ahead.

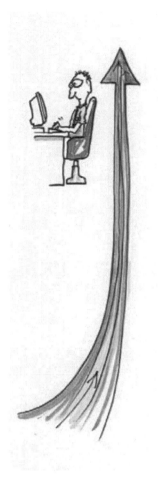

THE BEST ZONE: You are cooking! Well intoi the day, alert andf tackling whatever is thrown your way. You may have a little slump mid morning, but a refreshment will soon pick you up again.

THE BEST ZONE!

Thinking clearly, dashing about the place and dealing with the 'stuff of the day'. By mid to late morning you may have a slight slump, where you need to top up with something, but otherwise your system is "A-OK". Most of the time, we move up to this level, bob around a bit, then drop back down at the end of the day, into our beds then back to sleep. Up and down and up and down, in variable degrees. Stress comes in WAVES: up and down, and perfectly normal.

LET'S PUSH YOU <u>MUCH</u> HARDER NOW....

This is where things start to change, considerably! For if you go higher, due to much increased pressure, you start to enter **THE HIGH PRESSURE ZONE.**...

You are probably 'plate spinning' here, with little time and lots of tasks and demands to satisfy! YOU ARE BUILT TO DO THIS, but *ONLY FOR A SHORT PERIOD OF TIME!* Think back again to prehistory: you were designed to deal with an approaching tiger or threat. You blood pressure is high, your breathing is more shallow and faster, your muscles are tight (ready for action) and your mouth may be dry. A threat, in prehistoric times, was fleeting – a tiger fight lasted just a few minutes! You killed it, ran from it, or were severely mauled or killed! Today, there is no tiger, but there are emails, meetings, targets, tasks, time constraints and bosses. These have a nasty habit of going on for days, months and more! **Do not stay IN THIS ZONE FOR LONG!**

UH-OH! This is pretty DISTRESSING....you've stayed in that HIGH PRESSURE ZONE for too long now

THE DISTRESS ZONE

The HIGH PRESSURE is not being relieved, and staying under that pressure is taking its toll. This is a very uncomfortable zone with many symptoms! If you sort the pressures you can come down into **BEST ZONE** again pretty quickly. Sadly, we often take no notice, and 'carry on regardless'. _Health is at risk if you stay here!_ Your body and mind are ending clear signals, but if you don't take heed you are liable to change further...

THE FLAT ZONE

You are now getting *ZONED OUT* here – you just can't go any higher. This zone is often due to being in the HIGH PRESSURE ZONE and THE DISTRESS ZONE for far too long, and ignoring all the warning signs that your body and mind have been yelling at you! You mood is often the first to FLATTEN out, along with your energy. You are exhausted mentally and physically, but you are attempting to "soldier on". The 'signals' that your own body/mind are giving you are clear: CHANGE SOMETHING NOW! If you DO, and do the RIGHT things, you can move back down into a more normal daily pattern, after a few weeks (sometimes months) of making changes. If you continue on this road, something is going to have to give! You are exhausting your entire system....

THE DROP ZONE (A VERY SLIPPERY ROAD)

Things are starting to slide here. This is a very dangerous place as the slide down can be so SLOW, you may not even notice!

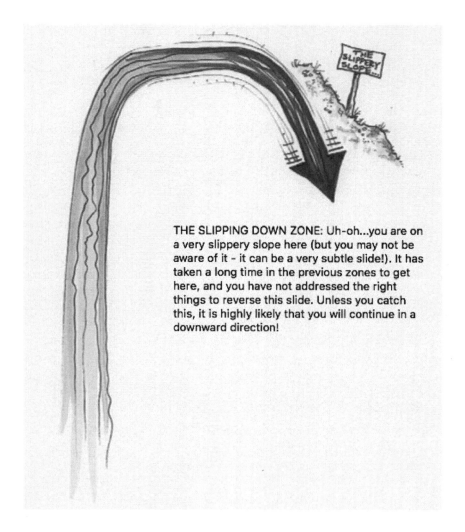

THE SLIPPING DOWN ZONE: Uh-oh...you are on a very slippery slope here (but you may not be aware of it - it can be a very subtle slide!). It has taken a long time in the previous zones to get here, and you have not addressed the right things to reverse this slide. Unless you catch this, it is highly likely that you will continue in a downward direction!

Take a few moments now to consider (and write down): **WHAT THINGS ARE LIKELY TO FALL, LOWER, DROP OR CHANGE (in any person) DUE TO UNRELENTING PRESSURES? Stop and think.**

Common things that start to DROP are:

- Energy – being tired all the time (even on days off)
- Mood – a lowering of mood, instability and irritability
- Confidence and self esteem – less trust in your own abilities (and maybe in others too?)
- Sense of humour changes– humour becomes more vicious/nasty/hurtful...or it simply disappears
- Perspective – blow things out of proportion or minimize important things
- Sleep changes – some have poor sleep, some can't stop sleeping
- Appetite changes – some eat more, some less. Weight changes
- Health deteriorates – physical health is worse/mental health is fragile
- Loss of interests – take up easy things that require no effort
- Quality drops – convenience takes over
- Pleasure – little 'feel good' factor and less laughter
- Aches and pains – recurrent headaches and various muscular pains (more consumption of pain killers)

Some serious alterations are needed now if you are to move back to a 'better place'. Not always big changes, but significant (and often numerous) changes are needed, now! Make those changes and within a few months an amazing change will be seen. Do nothing (as many do) and you are about to seriously drop even further!

THE **BURNOUT** ZONE!

Otherwise called the 'HAMSTER WHEEL' or the 'TRAMLINES TO DEATH' by some. Looking back, you may recognize that you've been sliding for some time, but not noticed it. You are now locked into a way of being that is characterized by *predictability, monotony, repetitiveness, tiredness* and *under stimulation.*

BURNOUT! You have been sliding for a while, and not taken heed of the 'signs' that your body and mind have been shouting at you! 'BURNOUT' is a bit like stepping onto a HAMSTER WHEEL...

IT IS THE START OF GROUNDHOG DAYS: *Get up – have breakfast – go to work – come home – watch TV – go to bed – get up – have breakfast – go to work – come home – watch TV – go to bed.......... Predictability and monotony starts to slip into daily living.*

BURNOUT is not Anxiety or Depression, but it is a **BIG WARNING SIGN** to these! Because it is NOT anxiety or depression, it is bearable, but it's not a happy place. But, because it is 'bearable', some people LIKE it in here! Some people like the stability of the hamster wheel, it is SAFE, and they know where they are: "Leave me alone!". For this reason, we must not always assume everyone wants out of here. Some spend many years, the rest of their life in here, and may be (in their own way) 'content', never wishing to upset the routines or challenge anything.

THE BIG 'C'

In burnout, we tend to feel *COMFY* – it's not that bad, don't want to rock the boat. We may also move towards *CONVENIENCE* – convenient food (take away, pre-cooked, tinned, microwave... food that requires no preparation or fresh ingredients). Therefore we fill our bodies with high salt and sugary foods, foods with preservatives and artificial colours: unhealthy food that WILL affect health. The other kind of convenience we seek, is convenient ENTERTAINMENT (it is EASY) – TV, mobile phone, games console, movies: so little exercise or physical activity, which again will affect our health.

As CONVENIENCE in whatever form increases, what starts to drop is **QUALITY**:

- Quality of diet drops
- Quality of time drops
- Quality of entertainment drops
- Quality of life drops

POTENTIAL ZONES are: **THE ANXIETY ZONE** & **THE DEPRESSION ZONE**

These are both **ILLNESS ZONES** that can be spiraled into via burnout. Some people move straight through from **DISTRESS** into these.

ANXIETY is a diagnosable disorder

Anxiety presents itself in many different ways, depending on many factors. Types of Anxiety Disorders are:

- Generalised Anxiety Disorder

- Panic Disorder

- Post Traumatic Stress Disorder

- Phobic Disorders

 - Obsessive Compulsive Disorders

Recently there has been a new classification of Anxiety disorder called **Digital Addiction** (you guessed it – an addiction to mobile phone use, computers, TV and indeed any digital device with a screen. This is sadly being seen in very young children too).

All Anxiety Disorders share some common symptoms, including:

Panic – Fear – Unease – Sleep disruption – Unable to stay calm or still – Cold, sweaty, numb or tingling hands or feet – Shortness of breath – Palpitations – Dry mouth – Nausea – Tense muscles – Dizzy spells

Depression is a diagnosable disorder that involves chemical changes in the body

THE DEPRESSION ZONE is the most common outcome of chronic burnout, but can also be part of an ANXIETY condition (Depression and Anxiety often co-exist). So, for some, the Hamster Wheel is NOT a place where contentment is found, but only makes them feel worse. An easy way to understand Depression, is to think of Depression as another kind of *scale*, divided into 3 parts:

Depression ranges from:

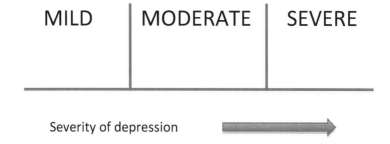

MILD | MODERATE | SEVERE

Severity of depression ➡

MILD depression:

- **Normal**. Mild depression is a normal response to bad things.
- It **passes**, is transient, coming and going in a wave pattern.
- It is NOT an illness, so **should not be prescribed** antidepressant medication (although it often is).
- Despite feeling awful, one can still function and get on with most things.
- One can still respond emotionally, to kindness and help.

MODERATE to **SEVERE** depression:

- This is **NOT** normal, it is an **ILLNESS**.
- It does not pass – it is **constant**.
- It generally does need **medication**.
- Functioning **IS** affected.
- Emotional responses are **minimized** .

Depression is characterized by a range of signs:

Often there can be a gnawing feeling that 'something just isn't right', with day to day tasks becoming more and more difficult, and an overwhelming sense of tiredness. It is not always "low mood" and "tearfulness", but it can be. There is most certainly:

Loss of INTEREST and PLEASURE

MOOD: Sadness – lack of enjoyment – anxiety – hopelessness - guilt

BODY: Tiredness – eating changes – sleep changes – stomach problems – headaches – chest pain

MIND: Difficulty concentrating – indecisive – slow thinking – forgetfulness – difficulty solving problems – difficulty in planning things.

Although in MODERATE depression (an illness state), many people still get up and get on with their day, masking what may be going on inside. Although the day is difficult and things may be slipping (and it is certainly exhausting) many do not know they are ill, and just 'get on with it'. So they don't ask for help, don't get help, are not assessed or treated. Sadly too, many who are picked up and treated, are not treated appropriately or followed up properly.

Once in the Hamster wheel, you have *CHANGED THE ENTIRE PATTERN!* You no longer need to go all the way round the pattern to get to 'the wheel' once you get up: **you take a short-cut!** Now, you get up, take the quickest route to the wheel, go round it, then return home and go to bed…..

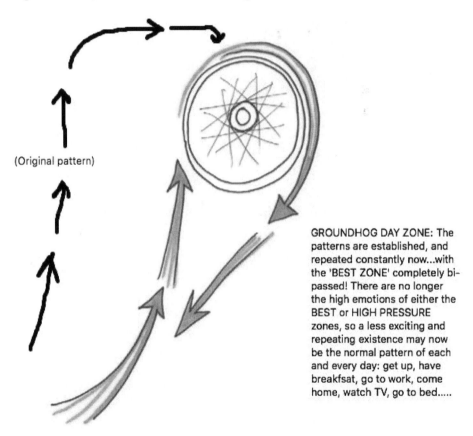

(Original pattern)

GROUNDHOG DAY ZONE: The patterns are established, and repeated constantly now…with the 'BEST ZONE' completely bi-passed! There are no longer the high emotions of either the BEST or HIGH PRESSURE zones, so a less exciting and repeating existence may now be the normal pattern of each and every day: get up, have breakfsat, go to work, come home, watch TV, go to bed…..

You have CUT OUT the **BEST** bits! By bypassing the BEST FUNCTIONING and HIGH PRESSURE zones, you've shut yourself down: just do what you need to do! This is why a lot of people who are burning out don't experience much 'high emotion' or excitement or passion (without copious amounts of alcohol!).

Some LIKE their hamster wheel – others feel TRAPPED by it.

So what are you going to do? We all have choices, and anyone can choose to stay on the wheel, become imprisoned by it, move onto worse things (like Anxiety and Depression), or start to make some plans to make some changes.

The most important start is to **ACKNOWLEDGE** where you think you are. A next step can be to be open about this to someone else who may help you through. If you have this level of INSIGHT and CARE about what you are doing to yourself, and most likely to others, it need not be painful to make some small changes over time.

OTHER STAGES TO LOOK OUT FOR as we go move through on this 'STRESS JOURNEY'. Here's the first stage, which occurs around the HIGH PRESSURE ZONE:

STAGE 1.

(The PLATE SPINNING stage)

Stage 1. is characterised by:
Fluctuations in mood, chronic tiredness & various aches and pains

Although things may be a bit fraught at times, tiredness may be blanketing over you, you still have your SENSE OF HUMOUR! You can still keep some perspective. You may have aches and pains....

At Stage.1 you are functioning high enough on the STRESS CURVE, to have made considerable *changes to your body and mind's chemistry*. This will inevitably provoke some **physical** symptoms. However, not everyone understands the **_LINK_** between their physical symptoms, and their own anxiousness. Men appear to be more likely to attribute any (stress) sign as a signal of some underlying major physical disease, rather than admit to it being caused by their own emotional distress. This is called **SOMATISATION** (A PHYSICAL symptom, but with no physical disorder present: caused by a build op of psychological tension).

Men are 4 times more likely to SOMATISE than women, and it can take up to 40% of a GP's consultations, daily. This is why it is SO important to understand what these chemical changes can and can't do, otherwise we might be seeking a physical explanation and worry MORE that we might have "something serious" going on, or that something has simply been missed by all the tests we've had.

Stage 2 is different! Your sense of humour disintegrates and you start to empty that (overfilled) trolley of yours., and it does not take much to TRIGGER things....

You may be starting to lose perspective and blow things out of proportion! At this stage you may be wandering around with an axe to grind...just waiting for someone to tread on your toes. If you are not aware of this, you may end up causing more pain!

A common sign of Stage 2. in the staff kitchen....

This person is blowing things WAY out of their proper size! The really bad ones put SIGNS up in the kitchen. The really *REALLY* bad ones LAMINATE the signs! This behavior is called 'SYMBOLIC BEHAVIOUR': this person is acting like this, because there is something wrong, <u>elsewhere</u>. Her trolley is spilling over...she is not emptying it regularly...**her needs are not being met!** If she had insight, she would SEE that she's blowing things up too big. *As a trainer, I do occasionally have a 'Stage 2. With NO INSIGHT' on my courses – these people already have concealed anger, resentment or bitterness, and they only need a small thing to trigger an outburst (usually me: I just need to say the 'wrong thing' and their anger boils to the surface. They need an OUTLET for their PAIN!).*

OR WHEN THE PHOTOCOPIER BREAKS DOWN...

Stage 2 is often characterized by regressive behaviours (child-like actions) that we all do from time to time. Some people can save this stuff until they get home (out of view), while others just let rip! Be careful you don't dump YOUR crap on someone or something! It can be uncomfortable to accept we can be a bit child-like (negatively) at times, but at least if we do, we can minimize it. Just look around you at the people who dump their trolley contents anywhere, without thought, simply to relieve their own distress, not thinking or caring about consequences.

A CAR DRIVER AT STAGE 2. (emptying their trolley)...

As you may see from this example: child-like outbursts, dumping his pain on someone else (who often does not deserve it), and spreading the virus to other people around by dumping his trolley carelessly! Maybe we are not just seeing individuals' burning out perhaps this is a reflection of SOCIETY burning?

Not all of us are shouters, swearers and noisy bangers.

Some simply withdraw...

These people are often not noticed when they become upset of distressed, as they are often 'quiet people', so no-one notices the difference. It's just that they've become quieter. So take particular note of the quiet people when they are under a lot of pressure...they may not be noisy big mouths, but suffer in silence. Such 'quiet suffering' can lead to horrible feelings of isolation, and the misleading thoughts that no-one cares, when they do. This is a slow-burning road to distress that others may know nothing about, so it is important to try and be as open and clear with others as you can. For others, do not always assume that 'quietness' is "OK" – some need coaxing and gentle prompting.

The final stage before sinking: we are going DOWN!

Stage 3.
Misery – Cynicism – Hopelessness – Helplessness – Give up

Commonly: Regressed (child-like) behaviours & lack of care

Stage 3. Is typically the start of 'giving up'. You may have lost the 'fight' or the will to say anything much, unless it's negative. Care is severely lacking now and often there is an increase in OBSTRUCTIVE behaviours. Insight may still be there (although it will be diminished), but when care drops then any 'change' is fought, blocked or mocked! It is not easy working or living with someone at this stage.

When any of us get to stage 3 we get a bit LOST...

If you are fortunate, then you may just have lost small things like your energy, your sense of humour or perhaps some of your creativity. But what happens if it is much more serious things like your confidence, your trust, your faith, your interests and your hopes or direction? Being 'lost' can fill us with a sense of helplessness and hopelessness, further adding to our (already building) sense of doom. We fail to see any 'lifelines' that may be thrown to us by others and find ourselves in a strange world....

LIVING WITH STRANGERS

We can become SO lost that people who have known us for years, stop recognizing us...

Maybe it is time to stop and ask ourselves: ***"Have I always been like this?"*** Change may not be wanted, but change is needed. It's not that there are no lifelines... it's more about not SEEING the possibilities and options that lie all around us, or believing that they are of any use. Some aren't, but some are. Is change possible?

So, can you CHANGE people?

People who are WILLING TO TAKE A LOOK can change. It is often easier for some NOT to look! It takes considerable courage to be willing to look at oneself analytically, but what can be gained from this is immense! If change were not possible, we would be extinct!

Often when we do look, we may come up initially with all the "bad stuff" about ourselves, and not see the other, more helpful sides that can give us more strength. It is often simply this process of looking, not necessarily changing anything, just taking a look, that brings ideas that can help us move forward.

IDEAS!

It is ONLY BY LOOKING that any of us can START TO HAVE IDEAS. Those who refuse to look at themselves, or avoid it at all costs, are either unlikely to change, or it will take them a much longer time to come to the realization that they may need to address some things.

This is why it can be useful to keep a journal about yourself: write things down that spring to mind. Write down useful quotes or things you see or encounter that may help you on your journey...don't let things pass you by. Writing things down can help us acknowledge things and keep a record of different parts of our journey. It can also help to show how we have changed.

A good cake doesn't just happen – you need INGREDIENTS. Good cooks are OPEN to testing out...

This important combination: having a **WILLINGNESS to LOOK** at oneself, and then actually LOOKING, can give us the **IDEAS** that can help move us forward. These are the **KEY INGREDIENTS** of....

Without these, little, or nothing will change. 'CHANGE' is often seen as a HUGE thing, or something that is very complicated. It is often not as hard as what it may FEEL like! Our thoughts and feelings can often TELL US LIES, making change a HUGE and impossible thing....when it may not be! At our lowest we may think: "What's the point – whatever I do will fail – no point in trying", but when feeling good we may think: "Actually, I think I'll try that – this might be pretty good – yeah...GO FOR IT!".

We are not up against the world, WE ARE UP AGAINST OURSELVES! It is our own INTERNAL DIALOGUE that is often our worst enemy. The battle is within...so we need to look INSIDE.

ASK YOURSELF: "AM I A FULLY BAKED HUMAN BEING, INCAPABLE OF ANY FURTHER CHANGE IN ANYTHING?"

It can be easy to 'sabotage' our own way forward!

It may be that we have programmed ourselves that nothing is worth trying for anymore, or that we are simply not capable of changing anything anymore. It can also be about timing: is it 'the right time' to consider altering some things? What we feel and think has a huge impact on what we do in the end:

- Feeling or thinking we can't do something does not mean we can't...we just THINK we can't, or FEEL we can't. Maybe we could try to prove ourselves wrong?
- Thinking or feeling we are hopeless, does not mean we ARE hopeless!
- Feeling or thinking we are stupid, does not mean we ARE stupid! We may feel it, and repeatedly tell ourselves it, but maybe it's time to prove otherwise?
- We may feel incapable – it doesn't mean we are!
- We may think that others are smarter than us – it doesn't mean they are!

OUR THOUGHTS & FEELINGS CAN TELL US LIES...maybe it is time to start showing (ourselves) that what we are THINKING and FEELING is NOT accurate, and not just accepting it. Accepting all that is bad is simply sinking into mud...it is never "All bad", just bits of it. Maybe it is more realistic to think: "Yes, bit of this are not good...but maybe it is worth trying a few things differently, and with some help, maybe?"

"You are NOT a fully baked human – ALL of us are capable of change. It is about CHOOSING and LOOKING".

Take a look at the 3 stages of burnout. Can you work out what **YOUR** signs are at each of these stages? Become familiar with your own signs, and maybe even work out others too (but it might be best to keep this to yourself, for now!).......

Now, keeping these 3 stages in your mind's eye, let us take a look at some of the people you WORK or LIVE with, and overlay these 3 stages on the types you come across.....

INNOVATORS!

These people are often 'Stage 1.' plate spinners. ...

INNOVATOR
(Stage 1. Plate spinners)

Innovators are generally nice, with creative ideas, a lot of energy, and willing to help. Innovators want to know more and come up with ideas that challenge things. Often with the capability of seeing another viewpoint, they question things and suggest ideas. They are often NEWER to the organization! They are not quite sizzling (like many others perhaps?) and still manage a smile and a friendly greeting.

LATE ADOPTERS!

Then you get the next lot, who are dipping in and out of **Stage 2**. and a good bit more worn down....

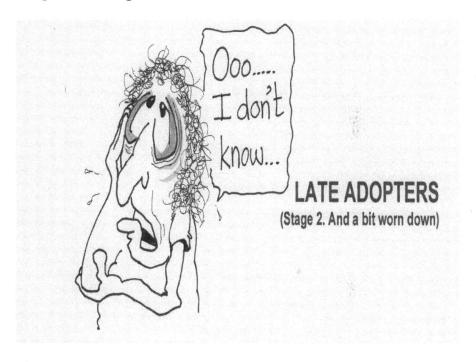

LATE ADOPTERS
(Stage 2. And a bit worn down)

These are people who have been in the system for much longer, and although we need them, they are a bit more reluctant to adopt change (usually because they've had so much of it!). These are called **LATE ADDOPTERS** (of change): more drained, a bit overwhelmed at times and pretty worn out. They will take on new things, but are harder to convince. They know how things work, and something is keeping them there (often medication)! <u>**Good teams need the INNOVATORS and the LATE ADOPTERS**</u>.

It is the last lot that causes the problems....

LAGGARDS!

These people are often dipping in and out of **Stage 3** and possibly Stage 49!

LAGGARDS
(Stage 3. and beyond!)

LAGGARDS are highly resistant to ANY change, and will often **block**, **obstruct** or (worse still) **sabotage** any change! You may hear the familiar cries from these people, such as:

"You can try it….but it will FAIL!" or "I've been here since 1896…I know best!"

You only need ONE 'Laggard' in a meeting to spread a toxic ripple around the table! It only takes ONE of these in a team to cause chaos! It only takes ONE of these at Christmas, to ruin the best made plans! Laggards are painful: PAIN-FULL

Having gone through the '3 STAGES OF BURNOUT' and now looked at some of the (corresponding) types of co-workers (the INNOVATOR, the LATE ADOPTER, and the LAGGARD, maybe we should accept that most of us have **ALL** of these 'characters' inside of us, at times? <u>We don't just stay in ONE character ALL the time.</u>

MOVING IN AND OUT OF ALL THESE 'CHARACTER STATES' IS **NORMAL** FROM TIME TO TIME.

What is NOT NORMAL, is becoming **STUCK** in **STAGE 3 / LAGGARD** mode! Being stuck here will cause ourselves huge amounts of pain, cause others to leave us alone, will infect family and friends, as well as colleagues and teams, and have the potential to COMPLETELY DESTROY OUR OWN LIFE! Sadly we may not even be aware of some of our (own) characters that could help us. Looking inside can help us find them.

So once more, I would like you to consider all the different 'characters' that inhabit our daily lives: the *INTERNAL CHARACTERS* as well as the ones we meet throughout each day.

Some of these internal characters are **GOOD** for us and for others around us. Other character states are not so good, and may be SELF-DESTRUCTIVE and capable of making our own lives more difficult: filling our hearts with huge amounts of 'bad' emotions and seemingly able to make us behave in ways that we know, somewhere in ourselves, are not who we truly are....

Getting more CONTROL over SOME of these characters, is essential if we are to MANAGE OUR STRESS better, which means we have to LOOK a bit closer to what is inside.

UNDERSTANDING OUR DIFFERENT PSYCHOLOGICAL STATES...OUR DIFFERENT 'INTERNAL CHARACTERS'

Getting to know ourselves better, and understanding why others behave the way they do, is a fascinating but sometimes difficult process. **UNDERSTANDING gives us POWER**: the *power* to **learn to control** some of our own internal characters (the ones that cause us so much discomfort). This is a skill that can be acquired by anyone willing to practice at it, but it is also a lot of fun using and applying it, so see this as an on-going **'Life Skill'** that just needs playing with.

Spotting danger is a skill...

The danger may come from **OUTSIDE**...but it may also come from **WITHIN**: others can hurt us, but we can do it all by ourselves!

THE GLASGOW MODEL!

The model I am basing this on is called **Transactional Analysis** (or T.A.), but for the sake of this book, I am abridging it considerably by adopting the Glasgow model. This model is basically saying that there are indeed, many different characters in our head, but they are GROUPED into very *specific types of characters*:

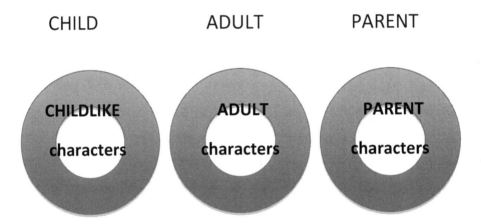

So, inside of us all are GROUPS of different characters. When we are IN one of these groups, we **think**, **feel** and **act** like that character state.: We are not just ONE character: we are DOZENS!

WE HAVE *MULTIPLE* POSITIVE CHILD STATES INSIDE.

WE HAVE *MULTIPLE* NEGATIVE CHILD STATES INSIDE.

WE HAVE *MULTIPLE* ADULT STATES INSIDE.

WE HAVE *MULTIPLE* POSITIVE PARENT STATES INSIDE.

WE HAVE *MULTIPLE* NEGATIVE PARENT STATES INSIDE.

Some states HELP and some DON'T HELP.

Within some of these groups there are quite ***different versions*** of these states, so let's now divide these groups into more detailed ones: the 3 groups are now subdivided, in parts, into 5 groups...

1.   2.   3.   4.   5.

SO THERE ARE **5** GROUPS OF CHARACTERS INSIDE OF US

CHILD (2 sets): positive/negative, ADULT (one set),
PARENT (2 sets): positive/negative = **5 sets**

CLARIFYING THE INDIVIDUAL CHARACTERISTICS:

ALL OF US HAVE EACH OF THE 5 GROUPS OF 'INTERNAL CHARACTERS', to a greater, or lesser extent:

So, in fact, some groups (CHILD and PARENT) are split into two groups of POSITIVE and NEGATIVE: Positive characteristics are ones that are good for us, Negative ones are not so, but we each have a MIX of all of these to some extent. In summary: we have 5 groups of characters in our heads, and now need to make some sense of what these groups are, and what characteristics are in each group, then apply them.

Exercise suggestion:

It can be useful, at this point, to write down (BEFORE reading the next part) what your own initial thoughts are about the characteristics you THINK, may be in each of these 5 groups? See if you can come up with 5 or 6 characteristics, in each of the following 5 groups, even if it's just a guess. Then see how close you are afterwards. So take a few minutes, and just write, off the top of your head, what you think may be the characteristics of....

POSITIVE CHILD CHARACTERISTICS........(list)?

NEGATIVE CHILD CHARACTERISTICS......(list)?

ADULT CHARACTERISTICS......................(list)?

POSITIVE PARENT CHARACTERISTICS.....(list)?

NEGATIVE PARENT CHARACTERISTICS....(list)?

Getting to know the characters INSIDE OUR HEADS:

As we go through these 'internal characters' you will immediately start to recognize certain people, including yourself, in these, which is fine....just don't get too alarmed! Remember, we ALL have some of these in each of us, but the effects and influences are different. If you have written something down before this section, you can you can now compare your own notes and see how close you were. It may be worth reminding you that these groups exist in EVERYONE regardless of age or gender.

TYPICAL CHARACTERISTICS OF EACH of the 5 GROUPS (compare these with your own notes):

CHILD (highly emotional) General: Child-like

characteristics that are easily recognized in all children, but some people have more, or less of these. CHILD characters can be both helpful and endearing, or irritating and embarrassing!

1. Positive CHILD: Playful and energetic, creative and adventurous, always asking questions and seeking knowledge. Full of fun, laughing and smiling, playing lots of different games and engaging with many different types of people. Highly spontaneous and uninhibited, with a thirst for 'new' things. Showing love by cuddling and saying it out loud (often to the embarrassment of others! Exploring and testing out. Generous and giving. Love is tactile and demonstrative. Living life to the full and in the moment

2. Negative CHILD: Tantrums with shouting and screaming. Extreme shyness and poor social skills, and perhaps a reluctance (or stubbornness) to try something. Pushing the limits too far and not knowing when to stop. Poor self-control . Aggressive; **a)** physically and verbally (to others), and **b)** to oneself (self-hurt). Devious, lying and cheating, never taking responsibility for own actions. Little guilt or remorse and poor moral self control. Over sensitive and over reacting. Tells tales and name-calling. Manipulative. Self-absorbed (ME-ME-ME). Rude and immature.

3. ADULT (not emotional at all) General: This is a unique

set of characters that are more logical and analytical than emotional. This STOPS...and THINKS. Inwardly digests what is going on and works problems out. Strategic planning and problem solving, but standing back and taking things in before reacting. Factual, serious and academic. These characters are a bit like having your own, built-in Mr. Spock! For those of you who have NO IDEA about Mr. Spock, may I suggest looking at an episode of the ORIGINAL Star Trek! Now, a WORD OF **WARNING:** Don't stay in ADULT MODE for too long, for if you do, you are very likely to become a BORING FART. **Take heed of this!**

PARENT (highly emotional) General: Parental

characteristics, some good, some not so. You do not need to BE a parent to have these, as you will often see young children displaying some of these.

4. Positive PARENT: Nurturing and protective, proud of ones own, and others achievements. Guiding and knowledgeable, using experience and wisdom. Listens, negotiates and compromises when necessary. A good role model and shows leadership skills. A clear communicator with a good set of rules and boundaries. Good moral judgment and holds a dignified stance. Patient, understanding and flexible. Able to see a true perspective.

5. Negative PARENT: Overbearing and controlling, with little (or no) compromise: rigid and blinkered. Domineering and bullying, with a tendency to abuse power, rank, status, people or money. Status is very important, so materialism feeds these characters, with the need to impress by what is owned. Cynical, miserable and complaining, holding resentments towards others they don't agree with or like. Punishing and passively aggressive. Capable of extreme emotional coldness. Arrogant, over-inflated opinion of oneself, snobbish and egotistical. Size matters! Inadequate. Cleverly manipulative. Belittling. Insincere. Punishing.

This is just a brief summary, to give you an idea of what sort of characteristics are in each of the 5 groups. Try taking 5 or 10 minutes and write down:

Suggested exercise A. What characteristics do **YOU** think you may have in each of the 5 groups:

1) MY 'positive child' characters?

2) MY 'negative child' characters?

3) My 'adult' characters?

4) My 'positive parent' characters?

5) My 'negative parent characters?

Suggested exercise B. What characteristics (from the above 5 groups) do you RECOGNISE in people you know?

Now have fun with this....

Over the next few hours and days, practice, in your head, SPOTTING THE CHARACTERS you encounter – it can be extremely entertaining, as well as a means to learning the principles of T.A. Play with it for a while. You won't always be correct, but that's OK (POSITIVE PARENT giving you permission to mess up here!). WATCH AND LEARN and you might even find that you can, by understanding, work people out better and react slightly better too, as well as reigning in some of those characters you find yourself moving into... the ones that don't do you any good.

Look INSIDE YOUR DRAINS!

'DRAINS' are people who are DRAINING!. Thinking of a few DRAINS that you know, or have known in the past, just list down the CHARACTERISTICS that spring to mind? Try, as you do this, to pinpoint WHICH PART OF THE MODEL (the 5 groups) these characteristics come from in DRAINS that you've known (or still know)?

- We can ALL be draining at times, some people more than others.
- DRAINS (be it yourself, or others) are usually functioning in negative child, adult (for long periods), or negative parent. They are not happy bunnies!
- If you meet a DRAIN, and you are NOT in drain-mode, they don't like that! So they will try *ANYTHING* to pull you over to their own *dark side*: they will say something or do something to try and MOVE you!
- When anyone is in **DRAIN-MODE**, they are draining themself and others, and are in a place that is likely to be unpleasant and not coping so well.

Now warm yourself on YOUR RADIATORS!

RADIATORS are people who help you to feel better and energized. Think of some people you know, or have known, that, whenever you are with them, you feel BETTER? What characteristics spring to mind (and can you pin these onto the T.A. model: which of the 5 groups do their characteristics come from)?

- RADIATORS tend to be in either positive child, adult (for short doses!) or positive parent.
- When YOU are in RADIATOR MODE you WILL be radiating something that is good for those around you, including yourself.
- No one can stay in RADIATOR mode, but recognize that this place is somewhere where you are likely to be more at rest, happier or coping better. It is a place of refuge at times of hardship. Learn to use it more for yourself.
- Most good radiators are quiet. LOUD 'radiators' may in fact be, DRAINS in a radiator's clothing!

WHEN WE START TO BURN OUT we often LOSE THE RADIATORS in ourselves, and in others! We LOSE our positive child, our sensible adult, and our positive parent characters. When we get near, or jump onto that hamster wheel, just think of how we feel, what we think and how we start behaving...

E.G. 'There's nothing I can do" (negative parent)

"Leave me alone!!!" (negative child)

Just consider the *inner dialogue* we can enter into when on the wheel, or sliding down towards it: we become dominated by DRAIN-thinking, DRAIN-emotions, and DRAIN-behaviours, some requiring HUGE amounts of alcohol to "feel good". Maybe it's time to recognize: WHAT ARE YOU DOING, OR NOT DOING TO YOURSELF? It can be tough to break out of these habits, but it IS possible, even for moments of time. Try it.

Playground games...and having **MORE CONTROL**!

There are constant 'games' at play from those around us. Take a bit of time and consider the effects of those you regularly encounter: who are these people, how do they interact with you, what effects do they have upon you, how do they talk to you, what do they do with you, how do their actions and mood affect you? Transactional Analysis is a model that can help teach us to STOP...then THINK (adult)...PAUSE...and TAKE MORE CONTROL: reduce others control over you by working out what they are trying to do, and how? <u>You take the steering wheel!</u> It is a skill, try it...

Occasionally, try and *intercept* yourself – *CATCH* yourself – then try and *MOVE* yourself into a different place (or group of characters), even for just for moments. **This is control !**

May I introduce you, to REG!

REG comes from T.A. and can help prompt us into considering where we are, in ourselves, and where others are. People who have **REG** are mostly functioning in *RADIATOR* mode, and are therefore pleasanter to be with, more inspiring, and they are coping generally better. People who do <u>NOT</u> have **REG,** are often in *DRAIN* mode, and may be draining themselves and draining others around them. Not having **REG** often means you are not in a coping place. R**EG** is also a basic requirement of anyone's **<u>PROFESSIONALISM</u>**.

Let's see what **REG** actually is ON THE FOLLOWING PAGE....

R stands for **RESPECT**. It comes from your ADULT self. Showing respect to yourself as well as to others, whether you know them or not, or agree with them or not. This is the most basic thing that bonds humans, and it is sadly diminishing across society.

No R = DISRESPECT (for self/others)

E stands for **EMPATHY** and CARE. It comes from your positive PARENT self. To show care to yourself and to others. To care about how you talk to people and how you treat them. To care about what you eat and how you run your life.

No E = LACK OF CARE (for self/others)

G stands for **GENUINESS**. It comes from your positive CHILD self. To be just YOU and not need to impress others by what you wear, what car you have and what you own. It is a very FREE place to be and reduces pressure on you massively.

No G = DISINGENUOUS (having to prove your worth to others)

So perhaps periodically ask yourself: "Have I got **REG** at the moment?" and if not, can you make a conscious move towards it? Consider too, those around you, and ask yourself if *THEY* have **REG**? What does it tell you about them? Use MORE REG !

May I ask you to consider the following questions:

In terms of your own 'internal characters' (that you are now more aware that you have inside of you), ask:

1). "What could I do with a little MORE of?"

2) "What could I do with a little LESS of?"

Some further reading and resources about Transactional Analysis that I have found useful (and understandable!):

'Counselling for Toads' by Robert de Board

(A wonderful little book that is quick, easy and fun to read. As you may gather from the title, it is about the characters in the wonderful 'Wind in the Willows' adventures)

'T.A. Today' by Ian Stewart

(A more in-depth look at what Transactional Analysis is, but highly understandable and a great reference book)

There are many books about the 'characters' inside of us that are not based in Transactional Analysis, but help us to understand others, and ourselves better. This understanding is gaining more control and power. I would highly recommend the following books as well:

'Who moved my Cheese?' by Dr. Spencer Johnson

and

'Fish" by Stephen C. Lundin

These last two books are gems! They explore attitude, outlook and how we can either imprison ourselves or find more happiness. They are also about change, team working and working with other people more successfully. Above all, they are quick, easy and yet illustrate key points beautifully.

Life ain't fair…work ain't fair…a lot of things are just <u>not fair</u>!

Life always has 'injustices'….

We could all make lists of the things in life that BUG us, and we would find that many of these things are indeed "NOT FAIR"…but there is often little we can do about them! It can actually be useful to make such a list: 'THINGS THAT BUG ME?' Then go through this list and work out the things that CAN be changed and the things that CAN'T.

Trying to change things that can't be changed is only going to make us more angry, frustrated, helpless and fed up (to say the least). Maybe it is more about <u>HOW YOU REACT</u> to these things that can be changed. We may still feel aggrieved, but if we can lessen the bad feelings, even just a bit, that is an accomplishment!

There are still too many MACHO attitudes out there!

There are still too many workplaces (and individuals) that have some ridiculous attitudes:

- MUST be tough (there's that *musterbation* again)!
- Must come in early – must stay on late – must not have breaks – must be seen to be strong!
- Be available immediately, at all times, and at any times!
- Don't show 'signs of weakness' (whatever that means!)!

WE NEED BREAKS....but PROPER breaks...without guilt!

People DO need breaks and stops, and not just to sit at a desk! How many of us have computer keyboards with biscuit crumbs and coffee stains all over them...BECAUSE WE DON'T MOVE AWAY! Try and MOVE, and also try to reduce the TIME SPENT AT A SCREEN (and YES, I DO mean the MOBILE PHONE as well!).... maybe some of us have lost the 'art of a break'?

We DO need to feel VALUED...at work or in life!

Some organisations have also lost the 'art of praise' and valuing their staff, relying on *blanket emails* or *newsletters* to convey how much they '...appreciate the hard work you've all done'! There is nothing to beat the face-to-face encounter with 'seniors' to convey value, but many places now do not do this. This sadly loses that personal touch that many people do value. All the more important for teams to value each other, and to SHOW it more.

Some of us need a CAVE ... a place to recover...

I know that I certainly need 'QUIET TIME' away from everything (and everyone) once in a while. Often, when we are surrounded by family, children or colleagues and noise....finding a quiet spot can be impossible. Whenever a quiet time appears, how often do we FILL our quiet time with MORE DISTRACTIONS (get onto our phone or computer, put on some loud radio or music)? For myself, I am VERY PROTECTIVE of my quiet time, and....I built a SHED! *I need a CAVE*. Do you have a cave, a place just for you?

The 'TOILET CAVE' is not always ideal...

Without a place to go for peace, we may resort to **long toilet times!** This is not always the best place to relax (*or carry out your deep breathing exercises!*). Consider trying to find ways to build into your day or week, real STOPs and real MOMENTS OF NOTHINGNESS. It has become very apparent that many children now do not know how to cope with nothing – after 3 seconds, they are BORED, so immediately get *Mr Mobile* into their little hands! Being "bored" is a helpful thing at times, to do nothing but perhaps look, listen and stop. Quiet is becoming a luxury item.... and as for OPEN PLAN OFFICES – *who thought of THAT torture?*

Please watch what you put into your face! I have tried to demonstrate the importance of our *'chemical balance'* in our body and mind. This chemical balance is directly affected by <u>what we consume</u>. So DIET is VERY important...

No-one ties us into a chair and FORCES bad food down us...WE do it to OURSELVES! The trouble, in part, might be that we tell ourselves things like:

- "What's the point" or "Why bother" (negative CHILD)
- "I'd never manage to change this...it's too hard, I'd only fail" (negative PARENT)

Start SMALL! In fact, *don't change ANYTHING*, for a bit. Just take note of what you eat and drink over a week...just write it down. Consider too, **WHO** is eating this food (your negative child or negative parent characters perhaps?). Consider getting your *positive parent* or *adult* to assist you at times: TRY IT!

DON'T FORGET ABOUT THE DIET THAT YOU PUMP INTO YOUR **BRAIN** TOO! There are some POOR BRAIN DIETs....

There is nothing wrong with a bit of 'TV GARBAGE' or 'GARBAGE SURFING' occasionally, just as there is nothing wrong with the occasional burger. But if you LIVE on burgers, I have a sneaky feeling you will start to SEE the changes in your body! If you LIVE on TV, the effects may not appear so obvious, but it DOES have an effect! Found yourself flicking through channels of crap for ages?

WATCH THE TIME YOU SPEND IN FRONT OF _ANY_ SCREEN (OF ANY SORT)....MAYBE IT IS TIME FOR MORE REAL LIFE?

ASK YOURSELF: " CAN I PUT THIS (TV/MOBILE PHONE/GAME CONSOLE ETC) DOWN....... OR AM I POSSIBLY <u>ADDICTED </u>TO THIS?"

Exercise is good....just don't make it TOO competitive!

Just be a bit careful of 'exercise'! Activity and MILD and REGULAR exercise is very good for us, and in conjunction with a better diet, will do WONDERS! But, some folk just take things a bit too far, and seem to want to thrash the living daylights out of an opponent, or thrash themselves into a pulp! You also don't HAVE to wear the latest 'IN gear' to perform in the gym or while out jogging! Regular mild exercise boosts your immune system.

Try and balance with some relaxation and quiet (remember that stuff...'quiet'?)

On the other side of the exercise coin, taking some time to relax, shut down, have peace and quiet is something we all know.... but tend not to DO. Once more, modern technology tends to interfere with our quiet time. Try to create moments, even just a few minutes here and there, to stop: shut off the TV, switch off the mobile (I appreciate that this can be traumatic for some!), close the door, pull the curtains and STOP. There is very little QUIET and PEACE around: having **'times of nothing'** in between the noise, improves **RESILIENCE** and **COPING**. You may find that many people who do not 'cope' so well, are the ones who also cannot cope with 'nothing'. There is a tendency to _FILL EVERY MOMENT_ with chatter, activity, music, events, people, work... not healthy!

Keep, protect and improve your sense of humour!

Smiling at ourselves helps keep things in their proper size. Not everyone may be with you on this, so be careful to whom you do this with! *I recently had a person (sadly in my home town of Glasgow) who had a sense of humour bi-pass! Everything was terribly serious, nothing fitted with this person's view of things, and sadly too, they didn't have the courage to simply speak to me to air their 'troubles'.... choosing, as anal (controlling) people do, to moan about it after! Still, they have given me some great cartoons to draw (which I now use on my course!). I don't think this particular person was in any condition to laugh at their own inability to keep things in perspective.* So sad to lose perspective, to lose tolerance, and be unable to embrace different viewpoints.

There are very few things in life that are SO serious, that a formal complaint needs to be taken out. This is often done by people who do not have the social and personal skills to deal with things in any other way, or (very commonly) they are consumed with so much anger, resentments or rage about other things that they are 'blinded' by their own desire for revenge! Most difficult things, even things that are worth complaining about, CAN be dealt with without the need for 'formalities'. Watch your own rage! If you find yourself doing a lot of this, maybe it is time to consider what it is you are _actually_ angry about, as it may not be the obvious things. Some folk just seek _compensation_ for their own sufferings!

Are you carrying too many **bags**?

It can be really hard, and for some impossible, to accept that they maybe need some help. Sadness, anger or rage can easily blind us to the fact that it is ourselves that actually are creating or maintaining (or escalating) a problem. Most of us can stand back, and perhaps view things from a different perspective, perhaps with the help of a partner or friend or therapist. But there are some who just seem intent on a destructive path that serves nothing and nobody, except as a means to relieve themselves of their own 'bags of pain'. Some don't have just bags, they have TRUCKLOADS of pain to disperse onto the world! Just look around the world and see how just a few truckloads of angry individuals can cause such devastation to the rest of us. No insight, no care and no respect, with a warped view of what is 'right'.

GREAT EXPECTATIONS!

Watch out for those imposed (or self-imposed) unrealistic expectations. These are closely associated with MUSTERBATION: Must achieve this and that, MUST get to there, MUST be the best or MUST be seen to be "Number ONE". We can become so wrapped up in the *must do-must do- must do's* that we only recognize that something is wrong, when we collapse with exhaustion! Learn to occasionally stand back, take a look at what you are doing or what is demanded of you? Who's agenda are you slogging yourself out for? Is this an indication that you are just saying "YES" when maybe it needs to be "NO"? Are you realistic?

Maybe it is time for some HELP....

Some of us are good at asking for help, some not. Some see this as a good, assertive action whilst others see it as a weakness. Perhaps it might be better asking for some support BEFORE we end up as a 'BUCKET CASE' sprawled all over the floor! Most often this is an informal and short-term thing to do, but sometimes it is an organizational issue that may need some formal management approval. Is there a culture of "It is OK to ask for help" or is this still seen as a sign of weakness? Rather than seeing it as asking for "help", maybe we should see this as COLLABORATION. This is surely desirable and be encouraged, not frowned upon.

Emptying your trolley by WRITING THINGS DOWN

This is a particularly powerful thing to do if you have UNSAID things: WRITE TO THEM...and DON'T HOLD ANYTHING BACK....

Just don't SEND it! This is a way to express your true and heartfelt thoughts and emotions, and although it may be tempting to send it, it is probably best not to – or at least, not straight away. After writing it (and I emphasis WRITING as opposed to TYPING it), put it aside. You can decide what to do with it later. It is common to struggle to start this, but it is also common to find that you use up far more paper than you initially thought you would use! It helps to empty the head (and probably some of the trolley too), and can release a lot of high emotion. Make some room for nicer things!

Breathing in the air of others...

Remember that we all **bring in an atmosphere**, be it at work or at home, an atmosphere that must be *breathed in* by those around us. I am amazed at what atmospheres some people bring in, and seem to be OBLIVIOUS (lack of INSIGHT)! Or they simply don't seem to be bothered about it (lack of CARE). We know that most of our language is non-verbal, so consider posture, eyes, facial expression, body movements and of course when the gob opens, the tone of voice, the words used and the overall impression that is being expelled. So what air are **you** bringing in... what atmosphere are those around you adding to **the air we all breathe?** It can be easy to forget the ripple effect we each have.

It is almost as if we all come to work wearing a T-shirt slogan: a reflection of what is going on inside perhaps? Some of us need to consider CHANGING THE T-SHIRT! Why is it that some folk just HAVE to share their 'stuff' with everyone else? Can they not hold it in, or save it for someone else? In this (narcissistic) world of social media, there is a tendency to 'share' – but often what is shared, is not reality. There can be a tendency to create an image for others to either be jealous of or gloat over. This works, IF you believe the images. There is a great capability to share good things, but there is also a huge (and growing) need for cruelty. What T-shirts are hang in YOUR wardrobe? What messages do you give to the world? Maybe it's time to make your world smaller?

Some of us are giving out other 'signals'...ones which others WILL use (and possibly abuse)....

Being aware of our signals can help us to create some new ones, should that be necessary. Consider what signals you would like to give out, ones that might help you more and help others be more aware of what lines you have drawn? It is nice to help, but helping TOO much (to please people or not to be seen as 'unhelpful') can quickly burn you out! It is about balance. It may also be about learning how to be assertive pleasantly, as there is no need to be aggressive or nasty. What messages do you give to the **social media world** about yourself: are they accurate or contrived?

Try out some ALTERNATIVE THERAPIES...

But they have their place! If I were this poor soul here, I would not want 2 drops of lavender and some tea tree oil...I'd want some medical assistance! I have heard of very few people who, once trying out some of these therapies, would not go back for more! There are lots to choose from, and often it may be about trying different ones out. Why wait to be pampered - **DO IT FOR YOURSELF!** Always check you are working with an accredited practitioner. Your body will tell you where to focus treatments on.

It is not uncommon to think that there is nothing that you, or anyone else, can do...

When we are particularly worn down, we can start wearing blinkers that shut out all the possibilities. There are always possibilities, and often the ones we have thought of are not the only options. When our thoughts are either speeding relentlessly through our minds, or dulled to a heavy stop, it is impossible to think clearly. Similarly, when we are filled with really overwhelming emotions such as sadness, frustration, worry or panic, it is not possible to clearly find our way through things. However overwhelmed we may be, it always passes, <u>always</u>. We may need to allow for time itself to work, or we may need the help of someone else to help us to regain our true perspective, not the distorted view that we may currently be believing in.

What **buttons** are you pushing?

We all have that 'SELF DESTRUCT' button in our heads, it's just that some of us only push it occasionally, while others stand leaning against it! No one pushes that button for us (yes people say things and do things that trigger us into a PUSH...but it is US that push it, not them). This is often something children do, but then learn the skills that teach us to use other approaches to deal with 'hard stuff'. What if we are not taught how to do this? Catching ourselves doing this is the first step, then learning to push it for SHORTER time periods (with less enthusiasm), as we start to explore better ways to respond. **Watch that button! It's YOUR finger!**

What about the people and things we CAN'T change?

Cognitive approaches tell us some important principles, that help us to challenge what we are saying and doing to ourselves....

Taking more responsibility! It is too easy to blame others or events for everything, rather than accepting we are actually responsible for our own thoughts, feelings and actions. This is something many don't like to accept: *I think, I feel and I do!*

Events may trigger our thoughts…but they are **OUR** thoughts (no-one put them there or inserted them. We created them). <u>Our thoughts are OURS</u>!

Events may trigger our emotions…. but they are **OUR** emotions (no-one placed them inside of us. We create them). <u>Our feelings are OURS!</u>

Events may trigger our reactions…. but they are **OUR** reactions (no-one makes us behave the way we do. We do what we do). <u>Our behaviours are OURS!</u>

This may be a bitter pill to swallow for some – but it is an important step to accept that these things are OURS! If they are ours, then stop blaming others, and look into ways to *STOP* or *BLOCK* or *MOVE* those troublesome thoughts, emotions or behaviours in yourself: finding a means to take back some control!

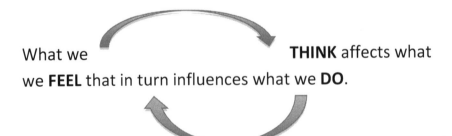

What we **THINK** affects what we **FEEL** that in turn influences what we **DO**.

So *THINKING* is linked to *EMOTIONS* which provoke *BEHAVIOURS*: THESE ARE ALL **LINKED** AND INFLUENCE EACH OTHER............and they are all **OUR OWN**.

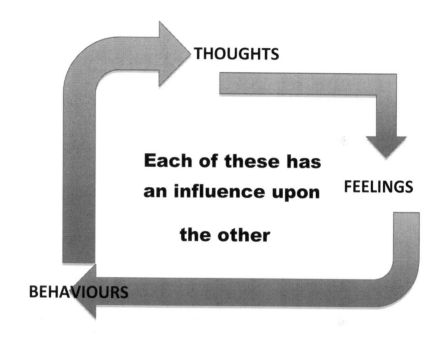

THOUGHTS

Each of these has

an influence upon   **FEELINGS**

the other

BEHAVIOURS

If we ALTER or CHANGE what we THINK, it will have a knock-on effect on how we BEHAVE and REACT. Likewise, if we change our behavior, it will have an effect on what we think and feel. EACH HAS IT'S EFFECT ON THE OTHER.

We are creatures of HABIT: we get into habitual ways of thinking, feeling and reacting. Most of these habits are maybe fine. It's the habits that are NOT OK, that need looking at, adjusting, or changing. What habits have you got that don't do you any good?

Understanding the link: ONE EFFECTS THE OTHER!

- Thinking bad thoughts will provoke unpleasant feelings, which in turn will have an influence on how we react and behave.
- Feeling unpleasant emotions will change how we behave, which will influence our thoughts.
- Doing things that you know are not helpful for you will create emotions and thoughts that will bring you down further.

CHANGE IS ALWAYS POSSIBLE IN ANY OF YOUR THOUGHTS /FEELINGS/BEHAVIOURS: DO YOU WANT CHANGE ?

THOUGHTS (T's) can be changed! Practice STOPPING a bad thought (Say "STOP" and try to BLOCK it)

FEELINGS (F's) can be changed! Practice STOPPING a bad feeling (Say "STOP" and try to block it/divert it)

BEHAVIOURS (B's) can be changed! Practice STOPPING a bad action (Say "STOP this...NOW")

We may need help to do this, but these can be altered and changed, unlike many of the things 'out there' that cannot be changed. Accepting the principle that **a)** *these things are our own,* and **b)** *that they can be changed* is a great step forward!

Consider looking into Cognitive Behaviour approaches. There are some great resources around. Often, learning about it ourselves, can be enough to help us grasp and use the principles.

The different **LEVEL OF CARE**

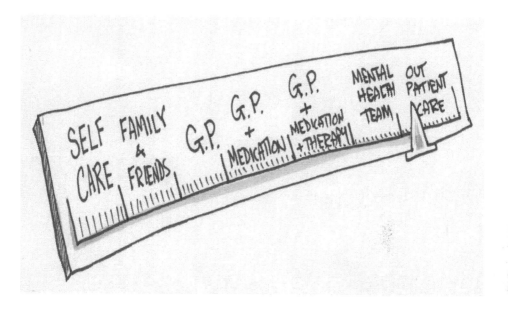

If we neglect ourselves, for whatever reasons, our health will suffer. If we continue to ignore a problem that is becoming worse, we may end up needing much more specialized help than if we had intervened earlier. Many people end up under the care of their family doctor, but only because they neglected the basics: **SELF CARE**. If we do need medical or specialist care, a positive aim is to look towards moving back down the scale, towards more self care. When helping others, this scale can also help guide us to where the person needs to aim for. Becoming over-dependent on others 'helping' us is not healthy, but any of us can move back down towards caring for ourselves, and being supported by family and friends, we may just need some help to do that occasionally. Sometimes we can convince ourselves that we 'need help' when in fact, we are perfectly capable of dealing with. Conversely, we may shun help when in fact we do need assistance. Where are you…. and where would you like to be…. Where are you heading?

Setbacks are BOUND to occur….

Setbacks are normal and, in fact, we NEED them! These are not 'bad' things, but <u>opportunities to learn</u>. Whether it is learning to drive a car, learning a language, learning how to be with a new partner in life.... there WILL be difficult times, obstacles or problems. It is about **HOW WE DEAL** with these setbacks, **HOW WE GET ROUND THEM**, and **WHAT WE LEARN FROM IT** that matters more than the problem itself. Setbacks are seldom pleasant but accept it is **ALL PART OF GETTING BETTER**. In fact, celebrate a setback: *"Woo-hoo... there's another setback!"* Just celebrate more when you see you've learned something, no matter how small, from it. Remember too, that some things were just not meant to be, so *moving on* is another lesson in resilience.

Wouldn't it be GREAT if the 'difficult' people in life would just **OWN UP** to their own wearisome ways...

Sadly, most don't. Often the people who cause us major problems are people who have more problems that the rest of us – they are OVERFLOWING with PAIN, and are more likely to go round emptying their trolley on those around them. In the words of Metallica: 'Sad but true'! Unless they have any awareness or care about their own behaviour, it is likely your wait for them to change will be a long one! Work them out and you'll cope better**O**

The STRESS VIRUS, in small quantities is fine and good, and even helpful. It gets us up in the day and improves our overall performance. So don't come down too hard on the wee stress virus: it is your friend, when small….

The problems occur when this 'wee beastie' grows into a MONUMUNGUS virus, and becomes a *BIG MONSTER BEASTIE*…

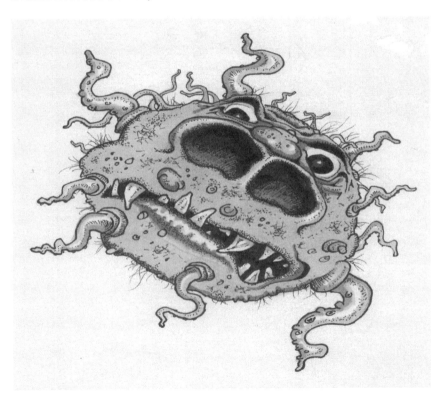

Immunity to the STRESS VIRUS?

Immunity to the virus has not yet been found by scientists, but then again, we do not want to *BE* immune from it, otherwise we would not even open our eyes in the morning or move (*a state we call 'adolescence'*). So perhaps we need to celebrate it more, but just keep it in check a bit better than we have been doing. Keep it in **manageable** numbers and watch out for the signs that it is growing TOO MUCH, for it will invite it's other *mates* along for a party, and you may start to have a major problem blossoming!

Watch for the subtle blossoming of 'little problems'....
which then grow into **<u>BIG</u>** ones...it's a sneaky thing!

Let us now move towards a little **CHECKLIST**!

This is a brief checklist (feel free to add other items that are perhaps more appropriate for you), looking at some of the KEY POINTS that will help any of us along the road to managing ourselves better. After all, we don't mind bending a bit with pressure, but don't break! Perhaps then, we should head this list:

The 'BEND…. *BUT DON'T BREAK!*' checklist

(You may wish to revisit this list periodically, to see how you are doing)

SCORE EACH OF THESE ON A 0 (LOW) …………TO 10 (HIGH) SCALE:

0___1___2___3___4___5___6___7___8___9___10

Range of INTERESTS	How full is your trolley
Time in front of a computer/laptop	Opportunity to talk
Time spent working	Quality of sleep
Time spent playing	Weight
Time spent doing rest or nothing	Quality of food eaten
Physical diet content	Time for you
Mental diet content	Amount of DRAINS
Amount of PLEASURE a) at work b) life	Amount of RADIATORS
Confidence and belief in yourself	Level of INSIGHT
Having a sense of ACHIEVEMENT	Level of self care
Hydration (water/fruit juice)	Treating yourself

Amount of tea/coffee

'Energy' drinks

Amount of alcohol

Amount of 'convenience' meals

Amount of sugary drinks

Amount of salty snacks

Time with friends

Break times during day

Time spent on mobile phone

Time spent in front of a TV

Amount of daily physical activity

Exercise

Knowledge about stress

Level of MOOD

Level of PRESSURE

Level of self control

Ability to ask for help

General health

Being bored

Looking forward

Negative thoughts

Negative feelings

Helpful people around

Tolerance

Practice taking little 'scores' of yourself, little measurements: "Have I moved UP the scale (on any of the above checklist), or perhaps I've moved DOWN a bit?". This can help you to make little adjustments along the road. Intervening at times, to alter something, or simply congratulating yourself for having a pretty good score! Monitor yourself at times to see how you're doing.

Making little alterations!

Never mind changing your entire life, family and where you may live...start a good bit smaller than this: *plan to make some little alterations.* A bit like adjusting the volume on the radio or altering the pressure on a brake pedal in a car – ***ease into small changes***, but log them or write them down as you do this. Remember: ANY changes, however small or big, must be continued for a period of time! It can be helpful to write down some of your own ideas about 'little alterations', maybe even go over these with your partner or family (try and get some help)? Remember that if you cut something out or down, what do you put in it's place? Watch what you 'substitute' things with! **Ease into it.**

Be carful about "suggestions" from other people!

Never tell a DRAIN what you are doing, and don't get these people to "HELP"! Only get folk who are RADIATORS to assist you. The people who 'know best' are often the people you should avoid....

(Hmmm...reminds me of some folk I've met recently.... on my course!)

CAN'T PEOPLE <u>SEE</u> WHAT THEY'RE DOING?

It really doesn't have to BE like THIS!

There are, sadly, a few folk out there who are not happy unless making others miserable. Remind yourself, that these people will probably never be truly 'happy', so steer clear as much as you can from them. Life is difficult enough without bringing more pain. We all are in pain, at times. We all share in others pain, at times. We all spread it from time to time. So in between, ease up off that PAIN PEDAL!

Life is too short

Now, talking of "life" – I would like to share with you a newspaper cutting (heaven knows where I got this from), but it has some powerful messages at the end of it. It reads:

"Bosses of a publishing firm are trying to work out how one of their employees had been found, sitting at his desk dead, after 5 days, before anyone even noticed. George, 51, who shared the open plan office with 23 other people, had quietly passed away on the Monday, but not been found until the following Saturday morning, by an office cleaner, who was asking him why he was working during the weekend. His boss said that George was a quiet man, always in early and left late at night, so no one found it unusual that he was in the same position and didn't say anything. He was a quiet man, shy and kept much to himself. A post mortem found that he had died of a coronary 5 days previously."

So, the **important messages** I suggest you take are:
1. You may want to give your colleagues a nudge occasionally.
2. Don't work too hard, because nobody really notices anyway.
3. There is a LIFE out there to be had, and *you don't get another chance at it!*

A final message from the author

May I thank all those brilliant people who have enjoyed my courses, as you have inspired me to continue. I would wish to particularly thank Marie Reilly, who has nagged me (sorry: prompted me!) to continue getting this book together, as well as my lovely wife Christine, who has always supported me through thick and thin! It has not been an easy few years and I am proud to express my humbleness to my daughter Michelle, as she has inspired so many through her own hard times. To my son Mark too, who has fought many a dragon to get to where he is. I cannot miss out my son-in-law who has been a rock throughout, and my other 'wee girl' Emma for constantly talking, but caring for us all.

I have learned a lot, both through my professional life and through 'hard times'. The people who inspire me are those who are not wrapped up with themselves, but who can see the good in giving. I have little appetite for the angry and resentful people who bring us down... unless they are willing and able to simply say "Sorry". Anyone can complain, and rant and rave or feel arrogant, superior and aloof... but not anyone can be courageous enough to address their own 'demons', and come through stronger.

Mental health is a fascinating subject, and I hope my book has kept you engaged, and that you take something from it, to help yourself and others. I hope too, that you realise that my cartoons are simply a means of conveying messages, and not poking fun (except to those who've supplied the material for me to draw naturally!). Life is too short not to taste a bit of it, so now....

..........get off your phones and get out there!

I thank my children for all the colour they bring to us:

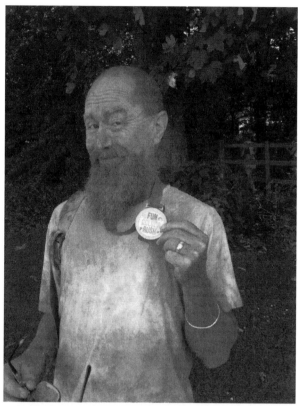

Go and get some colour put into your life

Martin takes his training courses all over the UK. and beyond....*boldly going where no man has gone before!*

Some lovely comments that I have received that inspire me to carry on. I thank you all. Here they are:

"I just wanted to contact you to say thank you for making the seminar day the most interesting and enjoyable training event I've been to, as well as giving me the perspective on my own depression and how I perceive it. Even counseling hasn't given me that perspective before. I'm so ready to tell my colleagues tomorrow about what has happened today. Many thanks for your help." C.H.

"I wanted to thank you for your amazing book...I read the whole book and could relate with every page. It's what I've been trying to explain to family and friends. It also pointed me towards things I need to do still. Anyway, thank you for an amazing book which I will be singing the praises of and passing to anyone and everyone to read." J.M.

"Today was absolutely amazing, both personally and professionally.....at my age I have attended a fair few study days, but today ticked ALL my boxes. You have a great talent when it comes to delivery." W.A.

"I came as a sceptic, but at least it was a day out of work. As you went through the day, I felt as if you were talking directly to me, about me! It just made SO much sense, some times uncomfortably, but sense none the less. I think I might have been one of the people you drew when I first came in, but I just wanted to say a huge thank you, sincerely for what you delivered...and HOW you delivered it!"   A.L.

martindavies.org

My business email:

Martin.Davies.Trainer@gmail.com

A final Government warning:

This piece of work, my training and presentations, is not for the faint-hearted! If you have a sense of humour bypass or need to throw stones, do not read this or book me! I only ask folk to have an open mind and be ready to look at things differently, and above all, to smile….at times, at yourself.

So I leave you with the historic salutation:

"Live long….and prosper"

Don't become like this…

This is Ms Bottom Face… a sad and miserable complainer!

Stress tip No.1 "Emergency STOP!"

OK.....'STOP NOW!' Before you explode. Catch it **NOW**. Say **"STOP"** to Yourself slowly, over and over. Repeat it slowly spell the word **S...T...O...P....** Slow-it-down....take a deep breath and slowly gather your thought. OK..good.

Try to get in as quickly as possible, if you find a sneaky little thought blowing way up out of proportion, or an unpleasant feeling becoming overwhelming, or you are about to indulge in a reaction that you simply know – you KNOW that this is not going to do you any good.

- PUT THE BRAKES ON ....NOW!
- REPEAT (for as many times as you need to) "STOP!"
- This is a kind of 'cardiac massage' for the brain: give 3 "STOP...STOP...STOP..." signals, and ONE DEEP BREATHE. Then repeat, slowing up a bit each time until you bring it down to: "STOP...deep breathe.... deep breathe...S.... T.... O.... P...deep breath...slows...slow...."
- This is about regaining control of an infected thought, a festering feeling or a self-destructive action.
- Use your own words or terminology if you don't like "STOP".... perhaps use "CALM" or "SLOW" or "CONTROL".... find words that suit you.

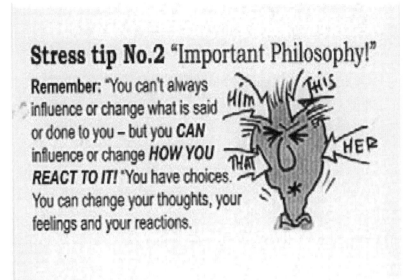

We are surrounded by many things we cannot influence, cannot change and things that may not be acceptable or fair. We must try and REMIND OURSELVES of this philosophy, however much it may run contrary to our gut instinct.

- There are ALWAYS OTHER CHOICES
- Are you 'BABYSITTING someone else's PAIN?
- Are you simply ABSORBING A STRESS INFECTION that someone else, or something else has dropped into your lap?
- How would someone else, someone you respect and admire, deal with this do you think?
- Is it HELPFUL or UNHELPFUL to react in the way you are...can you alter this, even slightly, for the better?

Stress tip No.3 "Deep Breathing"

Stop & sit quietly...relax...eyes closed...relax
Your shoulders/neck...relax your arms and hands
...now take a slow, deep breath in through
nose ...and HOLD for 1...2...3...4...blow out
through mouth. Relax. Take 2 normal breathes,
Repeat. Do this, with 2 normal breathes
in between for 2 minutes. Sit for 1 min after.

Get your breathing back into a slightly slower, deeper and controlled mode. Practice this daily, just for 30 seconds or so periodically. <u>Learn it before you use it!</u> Try and follow some simple principles:

- If you can, close your eyes, and don't change anything except your posture first – get those shoulders down; relax your arms and hands. Tilt your head slowly into a shallow circle (to loosen your neck muscles a bit).
- Close your mouth, breathe in slowly (via your nose) for a few seconds and hold.... for 2 seconds.... then release your breath via your mouth. Pause, and repeat. Then go back into normal breathing for a few breaths. Repeat.

SLOWLY IN THROUGH YOUR NOSE...OUT (FASTER) THROUGH YOUR MOUTH. TWICE

You are not only relaxing your system, but focusing your mind, but above all you are sending a very clear message to your brain that you are RELAXING AND IN CONTROL: THERE IS NO ALERT.... a signal to calm,

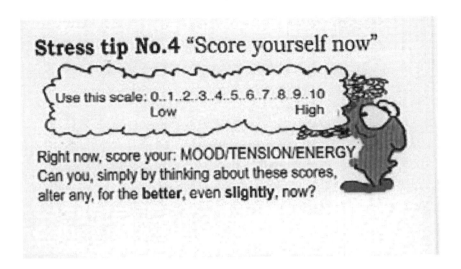

Learn to occasionally MONITOR YOURSELF. Whether it is your mood or tension levels, or your energy or tiredness. Practice using it on everyday things like:

- "Where's my appetite right now?" (Are you only at a 3, so you don't need anything...or are you at a 7 and ought to grab something?)
- "How tired am I right now?" (Are you at an 8 and really need sleep NOW...or just flagging a bit at a 6...maybe I need a drink of water?)

Try SCORING all sorts of things, just to get into the habit of scoring:
hunger/thirst/energy/pleasure/confidence/mood/quality of sleep/tension/pain (if you have a physical ailment)/relaxed/calmness/contentment/etc.

If the score needs altering (up or down), can you intervene and do something to alter it, preferably for the better?

Stress tip No.5 "Bend...don't break!"
You <u>can</u> do this! It's not life threatening...hard,
maybe VERY hard, but not impossible.
Rise yourself up – don't drop to others
(lower) standards...bend with it...bend..
but don't break. <u>Walk away with head up</u>.

We are not rigid structures, *we are all able to FLEX with pressure.* This flexing is a means to help us become stronger:

FLEXING BUILDS OUR PSYCHOLOGICAL IMMUNE SYSTEM!

High pressure, high levels of pain (physical or mental), distress and burnout make us more rigid, and therefore INTOLERANT TO FLEXIBILITY, so we are more likely to 'snap' quicker! When tensions rise, practice standing back, easing off the gas pedal, reducing muscle tension to move into a more fluid state…. bend with it if appropriate. We can't avoid all pressures, but we can learn to tense, then relax, rather than staying in a highly rigid state.

Stress tip No.6 "Feelings tell lies"

Your feelings often tell lies! Because you FEEL something, it doesn't mean you ARE it! You may FEEL "stupid"...it doesn't mean you are! You may FEEL "hopeless"...it doesn't mean you are! **Don't just accept (bad) feelings** – challenge it or argue it!

Watch those emotions! We are all perfectly capable of telling ourselves things that are simply not true:

- "Wow – I am just better than anyone else!" (Often not true!)
- "I am SO much smarter than they are!" (Often not true!)
- "They must think I'm such an idiot!" (Often not true!)
- "I am just pathetic - I have no strength in me at all!" (Often not true!)

So WATCH OUT FOR THE LIES that emotions tell us: we may FEEL it, but it does not mean it is an ACCURATE REPRESENTATION of reality! Smug and arrogant people often believe things about themselves that they feel (feeling superior, richer, more intelligent, prettier etc.,) when in fact (reality) they are not. People with less confidence tell themselves UNTRUTHS as well (feeling stupid, ugly, weak, incapable etc.) when in fact (reality) they are better than they feel. Learn to QUESTION EMOTIONS, particularly if they are making you feel bad: IT MAY NOT BE ACCURATE!

Stress tip No.7 "Have you got NATs?"

N.A.T.s are Negative Automatic Thoughts...
that fly into your head (with no warning)!
They clutter your head..lead to tension.
Watch out for them...try and catch
them sooner. Once they're in...
the stress virus gets a hold and
one 'bad' thought leads to another! Learn
to fight them – tell them to stop bugging you!

RAT's are BETTER than NAT's!

RAT's are **R**ealistic **A**utomatic **T**houghts – usually much more based in REALITY than anything that is NEGATIVE! *Negative thinking* will only ever provoke *negative emotions* and will result in actions (behaviours) that will only support how awful you are. So-called *'Positive Thinking'* may not be the best thing: as these (positive) thoughts may not be a true representation of the reality. Positive thinking may be (in theory) "NICE", but they may not be REAL. Practice REALITY THINKING more:

- Actually this isn't pleasant, but it'll pass (while positive thinking might say: "It's all fine!")
- Actually this is really hard (while positive thinking might say: "You're doing great...all is perfect!")

Learn to recognise what 'types' of thinking you are indulging in at times, as you may find that when you feel not-so-good, your thinking is either negative or it is trying to be 'positive'...but failing!

Stress tip No.8 "Ground yourself!"

OK-you're feeling pretty uptight now, so... take a few minutes: focus on one neutral or pleasant object (eg out the window?), and, for 2 mins, describe this object in microscopic/vivid detail to yourself. Don't be distracted by wandering...focus. Now!

We may find ourselves reflecting too much in past 'stuff' or looking ahead at things that 'might' happen, forgetting completely, the NOW. **GROUNDING OURSLEVES** in the **MOMENT** just helps ease some of the past or future stuff away...giving us a bit of space. Children do this constantly: LIVING IN THE MOMENT: they do not fret over the past or worry over the future. Sadly this is something we often may lose as we grow up. Perhaps we should take a lesson from our younger self: stop...and look...and wonder...look at the NOW...what is in front of us NOW.... the colours, the objects, the details. This is about EMMERSING ourselves into a few moments, of SIMPLY NOW. Get back to your worrying in a few minutes, but for a minute or so STOP & LOOK & SOAK IN

You may wish to consider looking into 'Mindfulness' more.

Stress tip No.9 "Panic feelings"

Panic feelings are just that. **FEELINGS**. They can't harm you however bad they feel. No-one collapses or dies from panic feelings. They always pass – it may take a few minutes, but they ALWAYS pass. Let them ...remind yourself.

Our bodies and mind are very capable of provoking all sorts of sensations that may appear to be on the verge of EXPLOSION! These sensations are built to do this – they are NORMAL – to convince us to RUN or FIGHT. Without these mechanisms going on, we would simply become extinct!

- It is NORMAL to have a faster heart rate – it can do no harm, it is simply alerting us.
- It is NORMAL to have racing thoughts and muscle tension – it can do us no harm, it is just alerting us.

The ALERT SYSTEM has always done this to us, and it was useful (in prehistoric times) to survive. It is still useful, but life is not so threatening now (no tigers – just work or life strife), and if we MISINTERPRET these sensations as life threatening, no wonder it makes us feel even worse! LEARNING about our body, what it can (and CANNOT) do is vital to reduce the fear. If necessary, find someone (who knows) to explain what is going on. IT CANNOT HARM US...it may be UNPLEASANT, but that is all. It is a NORMAL reaction, using NORMAL processes...but often in the wrong place.

NO ONE, IN THE HISTORY OF OUR SPECIES, HAS EVER DIED OF A PANIC ATTACK: TRUTH!

Stress tip No.10 "Quick relaxation"

(Good to practise regularly) In a quiet place, sit, close
Eyes...slowly (don't rush) relax your face...eyes...
Mouth...neck...shoulders. Take a slow breath.
Relax your back...legs...feet...toes. Repeat this
whole exercise again, **but even slower.**
Take 3-4 mins. After,sit quietly for a minute, then
slowly get up.

We are often unaware of how physically tense we are, particularly if we are sitting at a desk all-day or moving around all the time. Just as we are often unaware of how our breathing has become fast or shallow, it is good to stop and slow our breathing down once in a while. Quick relaxation is an easy means to keep a check on our body. Even just stopping, once in a while, to check how our posture is, to roll our neck around, lower our shoulders, shake our hands and move our backs into a better position.

Try sitting comfortably, dangle your arms at the side of a chair...slowly, over a period of 2 minutes, work down from the top of your head, working through each and every muscle groups...relaxing/moving/tensing and flexing. Periodically take a deep breathe. Try and walk a bit slower, sit back more when in a chair, relax your legs and thighs, and watch that GLASS SCREEN POSTURE (you know the one when you're looking at your mobile or computer)!

Practise-practise-practise!

Consider putting all these '10 tips' into your wallet or purse and carry them around with you. **Keep the 10 tips with you!**

Write-write- write!

Write when you feel you need to (good or not so)...get it out of your head. Consider keeping a notepad with you at all times, and perhaps at the side of the bed (as it is often night time that brings the NAT's). Keep a journal or diary. Use your diary to stash 'good tips' from everywhere!

Life-life-life!

Enjoy your computer stuff, just try and control IT...rather than it controlling YOU. Get out there and DO what humans are supposed to DO!

Eat-eat-eat!

Watch your mental and physical diet. Treat your mind and body with RESPECT and CARE...by all means have 'treats', but watch how many and how often. More QUALITY in!

R.E.G. - R.E.G. - R.E.G.!

Try not to drop to others standards; SELF respect – SELF care and empathy – BE YOU!

LEARN – LEARN - LEARN!

Understand how your body works – be wise: gain wisdom. *Knowing* is better than assuming!

Talk-talk-talk!

It's not always what you need, but use it when you can. Find someone that you can be truly open and honest with. Be a friend.... be friendly!

Look – look – look!
Use your ability to reflect on your own part in things: are you being a DRAIN or a RADIATOR?

Stop – stop – stop!
Get better at catching things before they get out of hand. Step back, PAUSE more before emptying your trolley (into yourself or onto others).

Learn – learn – learn!
Don't keep making the same mistakes : learn from what helps and what doesn't. Accept setbacks, but learn anything from them.

Play – play – play!
Allow that little child (the nice one) to take you over once in a while, ease up, let go a bit... play!

Smile more at yourself... life is hard enough!
Get others to smile... bring some light in!
Tame the I.T. in your life... get more REAL!
Encourage difference... don't stifle it in others!
Stop complaining... start celebrating, live now!
Things aren't important... living well is... now!
    More QUALITY... less convenience = RICH!

CATCH THAT VIRUS WHILE IT IS SMALL...

Have an open mind – be nice to yourself & others – accept others differences - embrace others views – keep your dignity – be yourself but be respectful – embrace life – smile at your own seriousness at times – play – don't cause unnecessary 'bad vibe' ripples – have FUN....

Share this book and your wisdom

If all else fails.... go and eat a banana

Remember your ancestors: they ate fruit, nuts and drank water. They made their own entertainment, socialised with real people and played in fields. Simplicity makes happy…. Keep it simple.

28981328R00093

Printed in Great Britain
by Amazon